DANIELLE DAMIANOV

e

REAL ESTATE SECRETS UNLOCKED

A REAL ESTATE AGENT'S GUIDE TO MASS PRODUCTION

$#IT YOU DON'T LEARN IN REAL ESTATE SCHOOL

BY

Danielle Damianov

REAL ESTATE SECRETS UNLOCKED

Copyright © 2020 by Danielle Damianov

All rights reserved. No part of this publication may be reproduced, distributed, or transmitted in any form or by any means, including photocopying, recording, or other electronic or mechanical methods, without the prior written permission of the author, except in the case of brief quotations embodied in critical reviews and certain other non-commercial uses permitted by copyright law.

Ordering Information: Quantity sales. Special discounts are available on quantity purchases by corporations, associations, and others. Orders by U.S. trade bookstores and wholesalers.

www.DreamStartersPublishing.com

DANIELLE DAMIANOV

Table of Contents

Acknowledgements 5

Introduction 8

The Power of your WHY 10

Goal Setting & Business Planning 19

Creating a Schedule (Focus, Time Blocking, Strict Schedule) 31

Working with Sellers 38

The Listing Presentation 42

Lead Generation 72

Working with Buyers 118

Designing Your Life 147

References 151

REAL ESTATE SECRETS UNLOCKED

--Disclaimer ---

This book was written to give you information exactly how I think and speak. I capitalize words and highlight phrases that mean a lot to me (which may in fact be grammatically incorrect). This allows you to see an accurate representation of who I am and my true writing style. Authenticity and transparency are extremely valuable to me. I really hope you like it.

DANIELLE DAMIANOV

Acknowledgements

I had a vision for this book for the past two years. I wanted to be able to share what I have learned along the way in my Real Estate Journey in order to help others succeed. I don't think there is anything special to what I have done or what I have accomplished. The truth is that we are always learning from everyone and if we just open our eyes we can learn something from everyone and every situation. The worse Situations are where true growth begins. I think one of the assets I have is to Learn from Other people and the ability to interpret what they say and relay the messages to everyone in my circle.

After Spending over $120,000 in Real Estate Coaching, I wanted to be able to share my knowledge with all Real Estate Agents looking to succeed. This book allows me to take what I have learned over the years and share it with the world. If I can help one person grow their business. If I can help one person get one more sale. If I can help one person Believe in themselves or push forward to see their dreams come true then I have done my job. With that, I must give a special thanks to all the people I have learned from along the way. I have learned and gained tremendous knowledge from the Mike Ferry Organization as I was a student and followed their coaching system for six years.

I want to give a special Thanks to all of the coaches that have helped me grow my business and believe in myself, as well as the many people I role-played with throughout the Country and the Mastermind Groups I was involved in. I also give a lot of credit to the other coaches I watched online or attended live classes and seminars. I have spent countless hours watching Youtube videos of Mike Ferry, Tom Ferry, Gary Keller, Kevin Ward, Craig Proctor and Motivational greats such as Ed Mylett, Wayne Dyer, Jack Canfield, Robert Kiyosaki, Zig Zigler, Les Brown, Byron Katie and others. As well as a special thanks to my family for always being there for me, supporting me and going along with my crazy ideas. We are always a student in life and my motto is if you Dream It and Believe It, you can Learn It and Achieve It! I urge you to read this book and go to my website at www.realestatesecretsunlocked.com to Download the PDF's that Go Along with this book.

So many times we attend a class, seminar or read a book and never implement anything from the book or seminar into our life. This is not just a book. This book is to be used as a working document to create the real estate business you dream of. Go to the Website and Download the PDF's that go along with this book. Be sure to really take time on each chapter and master each chapter to help you build your business. If you follow the steps in this book and really work it, you can go from Zero to Six Figures or from Good To Great in No Time! You Just have to Believe, Learn, Implement and Achieve. I believe in you!

Introduction

The best thing about Real Estate is that you can make $3,000 a Year or $3,000,000 a year...or more. It is up to you. In Real Estate you are the Owner of your own Business. The problem is that most agents get into the business and don't treat it like a business. They get into this business and love the flexibility, freedom, and making their own hours but the truth is that the Top Producers...the Real Estate Agents making $100,000 a year to $3,000,000 plus a year (Yes it can be done!) treat it like a business. They don't have the freedom and flexibility. Why? Because they know that to succeed in any business, you must put in the hours, work hard, show up early and be the last one to leave. Those are the ones that make it.

Now, I am not saying that every Real Estate Agent needs to strive to be making $3,000,000 plus a year, working long days/nights/weekends. I am saying that this business, how much you make, is truly up to you. If you are new to the business, think about how you want your business to be. Truly think about it. It is OK if you want to make $30,000 per year, work friends and family referrals. But if that is what you want, you need to come up with a plan and a schedule of how you will do that. If you want to make $200,000 per year, you can do that too. But you must have a plan and a schedule how to do that.

Your plan and your schedule at $200,000 per year will be very different from the person's plan and schedule at $30,000 per year. What I hope for you in this book is that I give you some ideas on how to grow your business. How to put a plan and a schedule together that works for you, and how to set goals. This book is designed for the Real Estate Agent wanting to make $100,000 plus a year. How you get to over $1,000,000 is up to you. It is up to your growth plan. It is up to the consistency in what you work. It is up to your dedication.

If you do the things in this book with consistency. If you show up every day to win. If you Work long hours, put in the time and are committed, YOU WILL make over $100,000 per year with these tips. You are about to build a business. Become your own CEO. Be the Entrepreneur you always wanted to be. It will be exciting. You will have challenges. There will be times you want to give up. But with any business, if you commit to getting through these challenges, working through them and realizing there is light at the end of the tunnel you will live the life that most others only dream of. Stay Focused. Get Excited and get ready for the ride of your lives!!!

Chapter 1

The Power of your WHY

    I am starting this book off with the Power of Why. Your Why will be the reason for why you do the things you do. Your Why will make you do things that you DON'T want to do in order to grow your business.

    When the market started crashing in 2007, I can remember sitting in the hospital room after just giving birth to my daughter and my husband coming into the room to tell me we just lost 20 deals in one day! I didn't know what to think. Since graduating from college, my world was Real Estate and Mortgage. We had made a killing in the boom and now things were starting to slide. By the beginning of 2008, the market was terrible. We moved our large Mortgage and Real Estate company to a small executive suite that had two desks. Most of our Real Estate Agents and Mortgage Brokers left the business. My husband bought a dry cleaner to make ends meet, and I went full time into Real Estate.

I had my daughter in August 2007 and my son in December 2008. So, on top of our business, our industry and our worlds crashing we had mounting bills, several mortgages we had to pay for, the expensive cars and everything else. I needed a plan, and I needed a plan fast. Luckily I had my parents local so my mom watched the babies and I went full time into Real Estate. I had to do things I did not want to do. I was pulling Lis Pendens from the County Clerk's office and door knocking the homeowners that were heading into foreclosure. I was letting them know I can help them with a Short Sale. I was scared…I was afraid of rejection…I didn't know what to say or how people would react BUT I had a HUGE WHY! I could not be broke and homeless with two babies.

As I mentioned, my husband bought a large dry cleaning business, a plant, 4 drop stores and 2 major commercial routes. He was in WAY over his head and the income we thought we would make from the Dry Cleaning business was non-existent. In fact, we had to put money into it each month to keep it from going under. What were we thinking?!?! In 2008 when the market was crashing…people had to scrimp and save, people were losing money, their homes and their jobs.... who would really spend money on Dry Cleaning? Hindsight is 20/20.

So that meant I was on the ground getting my hustle on. I door knocked 6 days a week. Within the first few months I had a lot of listings…all short sales. I was trying to continue my door knocking to get short sale listings and negotiate them at the same time. Driving to clients houses to pick up paperwork, dealing with the banks that took forever, learning the banks new computer systems for negotiation. Eventually, I hired a Short Sale negotiator to negotiate on my behalf (leverage!) so I could spend more time on what I did best. From there, it went to cold calling Expired Listings, For Sale By Owners, Just Listed and Just Sold.

The reason why I am telling you this is that my WHY was so big. I had nothing to lose. I was losing everything any way. At least we had our health, the ability to work, our family for support to watch the kids and I had my knuckles…for some good old fashioned door knocking! When your why is big enough, you will do the things you do not want to do. When your Why is big enough, you will do things that take you outside of your comfort zone. When your Why is big enough you will go the extra mile, you will go lengths to achieve your goals.

So, I ask you…. what is your Why? I want you to stop what you are doing right now. Get up, go get a pen and paper or a journal (even better!) and I want you to think. I want you to Brainstorm. I want you to dig deep and answer these questions. Take this to the next level. Continue to ask yourself why to get to the true reasoning and understanding behind your why.

Go to my site at www.realestatesecretsunlocked.com and check out the Vault where you can Download the Working Document to assist you in this Journey.

I want you to ask yourself these questions….

1. Why did you get into Real Estate?

2. What do you want to get out of this business? (Are you looking for flexibility, more money, time, freedom, what is it that you want?)

3. Why do you want that, or more importantly Why is that important to you? Dig Deep! Ask yourself Why to each answer 7 times. Take this 7 Levels Deep. Every Time you Answer Why…ask yourself, Why, again…

4. What is your Why?

5. Why do you want what you want?

6. What is your Vision in Business? Where do you see yourself in 1 year, 5 years, 10 years from now?

7. What is your Vision Personally? Where do you see yourself in 1 year, 5 years, 10 years from now in your health and personal life?

8. What excites you? Do you love to travel, do you want investment properties to create passive income, do you want to pay for your kids schooling or help your aging parents?

I can tell you that my WHY today differs greatly from my WHY back in 2008 - 2010. Back in 2008 - 2010, my Why was to survive and not get into a deep hole of debt and depression. My Why was to take care of my family. I believed in me and my husband and I knew we could bounce back. To do that, I had to push forward and not care what anyone said, get over my emotions, take the emotion out of it, handle rejection, negative people and just push forward no matter what happens.

Now that my kids are in 5th and 7th grade my Why is completely different. My Why is to pay for their primary and college educations so they do not have student loans, to live a great, healthy and happy life, to travel the world and create amazing memories with my family, to give back to my community and to have passive income and passive investments to retire at an early age and continue to live the life I want to live full of travel with my family. Creating different businesses that creates passive income excites me. Being able to figure out how to create wealth, passively through leverage and online systems excites me. My Why today has evolved, and yours will too.

But I want you to think about today and your future. Forget about your past. Your past does not matter anymore. Think about your future. Your why. Get excited! What is burning so deep inside you that when you think about it you smile, want to jump up and down? Some people will say that they don't have a "Why." They don't have that burning desire. Let me challenge you. If money were not an object. If you could do ANYTHING you wanted to do and money was not an issue. If you could be ANYTHING you wanted to be, and it was impossible to fail. What would it be?

Now, we have to be realistic. Obviously if you are a skinny 5ft. tall man, you are probably not going to be playing in the NBA. But if that is your passion then think of all the things you can do to surround yourself to be in the NBA. Sports Commentator, Analyst, Photographer, Nutritionist, Salesman, water boy, anything! If that is your passion or your dream...you can get there! With Real Estate, the cool thing is that you can make a lot of money in this business and still have the flexibility to design your day. So maybe your WHY is not to be a full time Real Estate Agent for the rest of your life. Maybe your Why is to make good money...selling real estate for now...while you make good money and work on your other passions at the same time so you can have the life you want to live and be the person you were put on this earth to be.

If you are one of those people that does not have a "Why," I encourage you to take some time at night or on the weekend or early morning before you start your day and brainstorm on you. Brainstorm on your life. Think about what you want. Where you want to live. The house you want to live in. They type of car you want to drive. What you want for your kids, your family, your parents, and you! Create your life in your mind. Think about your why and write it down. That burning desire inside will ignite and that will be Why you do the things you do moving forward. The only way to Grow. The only way to move forward is to get out of our comfort zone.

Your Life Begins at the end of your comfort zone. We MUST get comfortable being uncomfortable. Being uncomfortable means growth. You learn, you fail and you fail falling forward. You have breakthroughs and you become better. To grow, to push yourself, to get out of your comfort zone it all starts with your WHY. If your WHY isn't big enough, you won't do it. So, what is your why? Check out the Vault at www.realestatesecretsunlocked.com for some brainstorming questions on your Why.

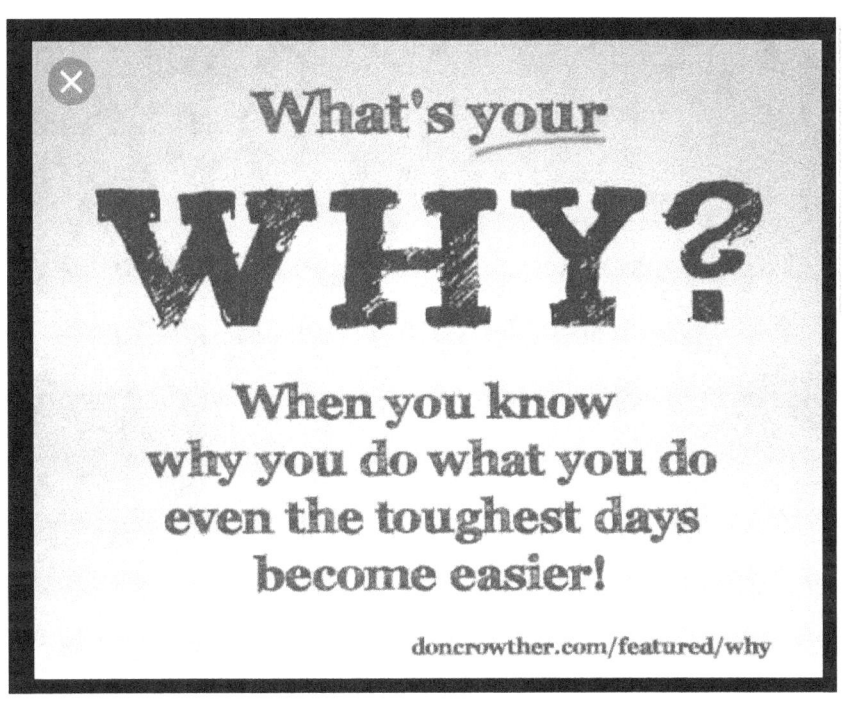

"The biggest rewards in life are found outside your comfort zone. Live with it. Fear and risk are prerequisites if you want to enjoy a life of success and adventure."

Jack Canfield

Chapter 2

Goal Setting & Business Planning

Goal setting and Business Planning is one of the most important things we can do in our business and probably one of the things we fail to do. If we fail to plan then we plan to fail. I think the biggest obstacle with goal setting is two-fold. There are three types of people. You are the person who has never created a business plan for your business, never tracked your numbers, does not understand where you are in your business and has no clear or concise plan on where you are going…OR…you are the person who every year creates a business plan for the following year, implements your plan in January of that year and never looks at the business plan again until October/November of that year to see if you met your goals. The third type is the Top Producers. The ones that have Specific and Measurable Goals, they Track their Achievements and Review their plan daily. The goal is to set a business plan, and then monitor and track your plan daily. If you are Person (B) that created the plan…you are a tiny bit better than the person who didn't create the plan at all. Here is the thing.

Top Producers track their numbers. They watch their business like a Hawk. They know where they are in their business at all times. They know their conversion ratios; how many people they need to talk to and how many conversations they need to have in order to get a signed contract and then how many signed contracts lead to a closing. They know their marketing costs and budget. They watch their Return on Investment (ROI) and make decisions quickly. They look to see what is costing them more money. Where they need leverage. What they need to stop doing and what they need to do more of. They know the 80/20 rule and what 20% is bringing in 80% of the business. They know they need to diversify and not "put all their eggs in one basket."

Top Producers run their real estate business like any other sales business. We have to remember. Real Estate is Sales. We are in a Sales Business. Not only that, we are selling someone's biggest asset, their home. Home Buyers and Sellers have a lot at stake. We must be respectful of that and treat this business seriously. Now that we know our WHY, the next step is to devise a plan. If you are just starting out in this business, the best thing you can do is to have an annual, monthly, weekly and daily plan.

If you are not just getting started in this business, then you must FIRST figure out where you are today. It doesn't matter what you did 3 years ago, 5 years ago, 10 years ago. Look at your numbers for last year and this year. Get very clear on where you are today. Check out the Business Plan Questions in the Vault at www.realestatesecretsunlocked.com

OK, now grab Your Journal and get a pen. I want you to write down:

1. Where are you at today? How many deals have you closed this year? Then ask yourself…is this where you want to be? Are you happy with this number? Do you want to do more and if so, how much more? Then ask yourself WHY?

2. How much money have you made so far this year? Is that enough to pay your bills and live the life you want? If YES…then is that figure enough to achieve all your hopes, dreams and aspirations? If the answer is NO, then get very clear on how much money you need to make in order to make that happen?

3. You can either create a Transaction Goal or an Income Goal for the following year. Most Top Producers create a Transaction Goal because they know if they make their Transaction Goal they will either meet or exceed their income goal. If you create an income goal and score a huge Multi-Million dollar listing…then you achieved your income goal. So, what are you going to do for the rest of the year? Most people will take off…But the Top Producers will work hard to double, triple or quadruple their earnings.

4. Where do you desire to be? What do you want your business to look like? Do you want a team of Buyers agents, listing agents, a freedom caller or cold caller, a marketing coordinator, etc. or do you want to add a little bit of leverage such as a Virtual Assistant and maybe a Transaction Coordinator?

5. What Systems do you need to implement in your business? Do you have your Buyers System down, Your Listing System Down, your Lead Generation System down? If you have nothing started then you MUST start with getting your Lead Generation System down. Without Leads you have no business. Leads are the Lifeblood of ANY sales business. You can be the best Real Estate Agent in town. The best negotiator. The best Buyers agent. You have an eye for

investment properties. But if you don't have leads...you have nothing.

6. Raise Your Frequency- Visualize what you want!!! Visualize yourself being that Badass Rockstar Real Estate Agent that you are! Visualize yourself driving around town in Mercedes convertible heading to your 5th listing appointment for the day. Visualize your life and what you want. You must be Pro-Active and not Re-Active. Before you can set a goal, you need to get very clear on where you are today.

7. Get another piece of paper- NOW. Make a T—On the left side of the paper write the word STOP — and on the Right Side write DO MORE; Now I want you to think about your day to day. What are you doing in your day that is getting in the way of bringing in more business? What do you need to STOP Doing? For Me, email is a killer. I can get sucked into email for hours. Is that you too? Is it constantly checking your email, checking your social media feeds, going to the gym mid-day, taking a long lunch, etc.? Think about it. What are the things that if you stopped doing them immediately and filled that time with Pro-Active and Productive things that you would bring in more deals or make more money?

Now go down the right side. What do you need to do MORE OF—that if you did more of it, would bring you more business? Maybe it is more cold calling, more lead generating, more lead follow, more handwritten notes to your past clients, calling your sphere of influence, leverage for marketing, etc. Get that list and start small. Pick ONE or TWO things that you need to Stop Doing…and Do More of to increase productivity and start immediately!

8. What is your 20%? The Pareto principle (also known as the 80/20 rule, the law of the vital few, or the principle of factor sparsity) states that, for many events, roughly 80% of the effects come from 20% of the causes. So, think about your business. Where is the majority of your business coming from? Is your primary source of business expired listings, a referral from a friend, past clients? Where is the majority of your business coming from? Do more of that! But more importantly…what are the one or two things that you can implement into your business that if you did it consistently would generate more income? What are the things that you need to Automate, Leverage or Outsource to bring you more business?

Napoleon Hill says, "A Goal is a dream with a Deadline" and Earl Nightingale says, "A Goal without a Plan is just a Wish." You must Set a Goal, Devise a Plan to reach your goal and create a schedule to implement your Plan.

Goal Setting - Real estate works in 90 day cycles. The biggest mistake that most people make is that they get their Business plan done in December and start implementing their plan in January. By the time March Roles around they are freaking out because they are behind on their Transaction Goals and income Goals. Some may be broke because they haven't made a dime in January or February!

Real Estate works in 90 day cycles so we must start our Business Plan in October. In Fact, our Business plan MUST be done by October 1st for the following year. We must start implementing our Plan by October 1st and create a 15 month business plan. Why? Because what we do in October, November and December will be our income for January, February and March.

Most Low Producers get caught up in the excitement of the 4th quarter. They love the Halloween Parties, Thanksgiving, Christmas parties go on vacation and don't push through the 4th quarter like they do in the 1st quarter of each year. Then they freak out in January, February and March when nothing is coming in. They work like crazy in January and February and finally pick up the momentum to see results in March and April. Is that person you? What would happen to your year if you had the same gusto in

October, November and December that you do in January, February and March?

What would your business look like? Would you THEN be on track to hit your goals...or possibly double them? I want you to remember this and create your Business Plan and your Goals...have them ready to go and implement by October 1st each year. You work off of a 15 month business plan at ALL TIMES!!! Check out my 3 Month and 15 Month Business Plan in the Vault at www.realestatesecretsunlocked.com.

Step 1- Set an Annual Goal (to include the 4th quarter)

Step 2- Work Backwards to set a Monthly and Weekly Goal

Step 3- Chunk your Goals down into 3 Month (90 day cycles) and then divide them into your monthly/weekly/daily goals

Step 4- Every Sunday night you MUST — Review your Week. Have everyone that you are calling and all of your Lead Generating Activities ready and scheduled for the week. Review your Goals for the week and write them down!!!

Step 5- Get an Accountability Partner — Find someone...anyone...from your office, a friend, a family member, your spouse, your kids, anyone that will hold you accountable to your goals.

Tips

Set small achievable goals, schedule wins so that when you achieve your goal, you get a prize. Include your family!!! Share with your spouse and your kids what your goals are and what you are working towards, and what that will do for them and your family. Don't Give Up!!! Your Dreams are right around the corner. Push through. Be consistent. Remember that consistent actions will bring results in 90 days. Have fun! It is OK to fail. Do not try to be perfect. Just do it. Do not have Analysis Paralysis. The most successful people did not start out being the best. I am sure they sucked at whatever they were trying to do…But Speed of Implementation and Consistency is what will get you there! Don't give up on your dreams. They are there to be achieved!!!

Business Plan

Your Business Plan and your Goals will go hand in hand. Your Business Plan will look at your business and see where all your deals are coming from. What is working and what is not working. What do you need to do more of in your business and what do you need to stop doing in your business? Where do you need to leverage to grow? Are you going to hire a Virtual Assistant or bring someone on full time? Where is the vision of your business going to be in the next year? I want you to look at your schedule for the next year and plan the following:

1. What days are you taking off?

2. How many days are you going to work next year (per year and per month)?

3. How much money are you going to make?

4. How many transactions do you want to do?

5. What System do you need to implement into your business to grow? (Buyer System, Listing System, Lead Generation System, Handling the Transaction from Contract to Close)

6. Who is your next hire and why?

7. What areas are you good at?

8. What do you need to improve?

9. What in the business do you enjoy doing?

10. What do you hate doing?

11. What requires more skill?

12. What are the current Lead Generation strategies you are using (Are those Pro-Active or Re-Active Strategies)

13. How much money are you spending on Marketing, systems (i.e. Top producer), Staff, Marketing, etc.

14. If you are spending money on Lead Generation, what is your ROI? If your ROI is not at least (10%) you must get rid of it immediately! Stop spending money on something you "hope/think/or may work" - Get rid of it NOW!!! Do you want to earn more income? Here is an easy tip…Look at your Current Expenses. Ask yourself, "What am I spending," or "What is on Auto Pay that I can cut immediately?" Make more money by simply eliminating expenses.

15. What do you need to leverage or outsource and how are you going to do that?

REAL ESTATE SECRETS UNLOCKED

The **Pareto principle**, also known as the **80/20** rule, **is** a theory maintaining that 80 percent of the output from a given situation or system **is** determined by 20 percent of the input.

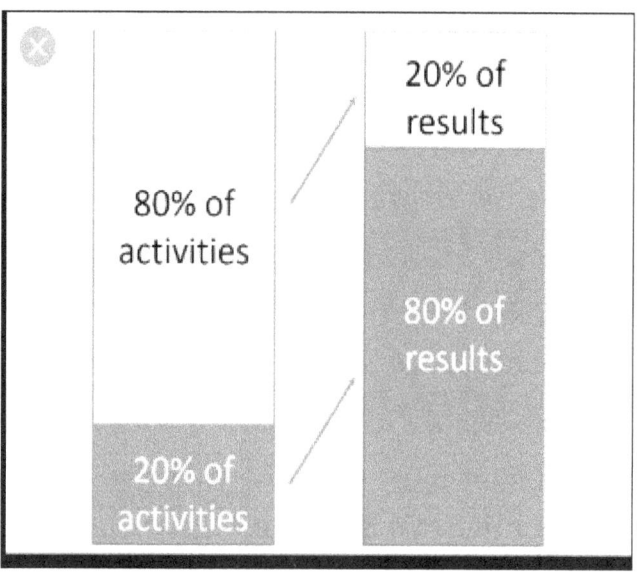

Chapter 3

Creating a Schedule (Focus, Time Blocking, Strict Schedule)

Remember, your day starts the night before and your week starts on Sunday Night. You must review your week every Sunday night. You must review your plan, your goals, and visualize what will happen for you that week. If you don't want to prepare your week on Sunday night, then prepare your week on Friday afternoons. Take a few hours every Friday to prepare your week for the following. Make sure you have your plan of attack. Who you are calling? Your numbers. Your schedule. If nothing else, you must master your morning schedule. Your morning schedule is your KEY to Success and it MUST start with Lead Generation and Lead Follow Up. Your

Schedule must support your goals. Be Pro-Active and Not Re-Active. You Control the day. Do not let the day control you.

Do NOT let ANYTHING interrupt your Lead Generation time. There is no Buyer or Seller in this world that I have EVER set an appointment with until after 11am daily. Period! Not One! Don't do it. When you master your schedule and respect your lead generation time, your business will grow exponentially. Having a solid schedule is the key to your success. You can Check out my Schedule in the Vault at www.realestatesecretsunlocked.com You need to find a Schedule that Fits Into Your Business and Your Day.

Different Types of schedules:

Strict Time Schedule
Time Blocking
Banker's Hours 9 – 5
Flexible

A Few Tips:

Foundation

Solid homes are built One Brick at a Time. You must Lay the Foundation for your business. Think of all the aspects of a Real Estate sales business. Lead Generation, Buyer Appointments, Listing Appointments, Price Reductions, Showing Appointments, Presenting the Offer, Negotiating the Offer, Contract to Close, Marketing Yourself, Marketing your Listings——Do you just wing it every time or do you have a solid system for each aspect?

If you do not have a Solid System for each…then you must create one. My tip is to start with a Lead Generation System. If you do not have any leads…you don't have a business. That is like a Doctor without a patient. He can be the best Doctor in the world, but if no one knows about him…then it doesn't really matter. You must have a system to generate leads daily. If you don't, you will be working a 2nd job to survive or joining a team.

Start with 1 thing…one system. Build it, Work it, Master it and Move on to building the next system.

Overwhelm

The problem with most people's business is that they are on the constant Roller Coaster. They generate leads. Leads turns into business. They work on their "deals" and stop lead generating because of Overwhelm….and then what happens? The deals they were working on either close…or die….and they are back to square one with no business. Do not be a victim of Overwhelm!!! If you get Overwhelmed, you MUST STILL generate leads daily and get someone to help you.

In the beginning...Yes you might work a ton of hours. That's what happens in any business where you are the CEO. It will get easier. The more deals you have, the more money you make, the more people you hire to do the things you don't want to do and the more your business grows. The minute you stop lead generating due to overwhelm...it will put you right back on the roller coaster, you will lose your momentum and be back at square one. Trust me!!! I was there! That was me and my life in my business. I learned the hard way! In order to consistently grow your business you must consistently generate leads, regardless how busy you feel.

Consistency

You do not have to be the best. If all you are is consistent, that will get you to where you want to go! Results take time. It does not happen overnight. Believe me, I want instant gratification just like everyone else but it doesn't work like that. It will take longer than we thought. But if we are consistent in the day to day. If we are OK with the Mundane. If we wake up, show up and take a Pro-Active in our approach we are ahead of 90% of the people in the workplace. All we need to do is find what works for us and do that "thing" 5 days a week. Consistency will get you there! If there is anything you get out of this book, this is the One Thing that is of the utmost importance. Being Consistent will get you where you want to go. Whether it is in business with your Business Plan or in Life with your habits, your diet, the gym. Consistency is the key to success.

Breakdowns and Breakthroughs

I used to HATE feeling Stuck. I mean…come on… who likes that? BUT now I embrace it. I know that when business is slow, or I feel stuck or something goes wrong it is an Opportunity to Grow. An opportunity to learn. An opportunity to fine tune. So, whenever I get to that feeling like the entire world is crashing around me…. I stop and look for clues. What is the clue here? How am I going to grow from this? I know that right around the corner is the rainbow. The sun will come out and I will be better than ever. The old me would freak out, possibly cry, go home and drink wine wondering WTF?!? The new me says …." let me take a step back and look at the whole picture" and ask myself how I can learn. How I can better myself, or my systems.

Believe me…it may take a few days or a week for me to really step back and see the light but it does eventually come and I am so grateful for that!!! Breakdowns are the Infancy of a Breakthrough. Remember that. Don't Jump Ship. Look for the opportunity. It is there!!! Even if it takes a while to see it.

Check Out My Breakdown to Breakthrough Chart in the Vault at www.realestatesecretsunlocked.com and keep it handy! Print out a ton of them. Believe me, you will have a lot of Breakdowns in the beginning (If you are truly working!). You must identify your Breakdowns, pick your chin up and create a Breakthrough. This is how your business will grow!

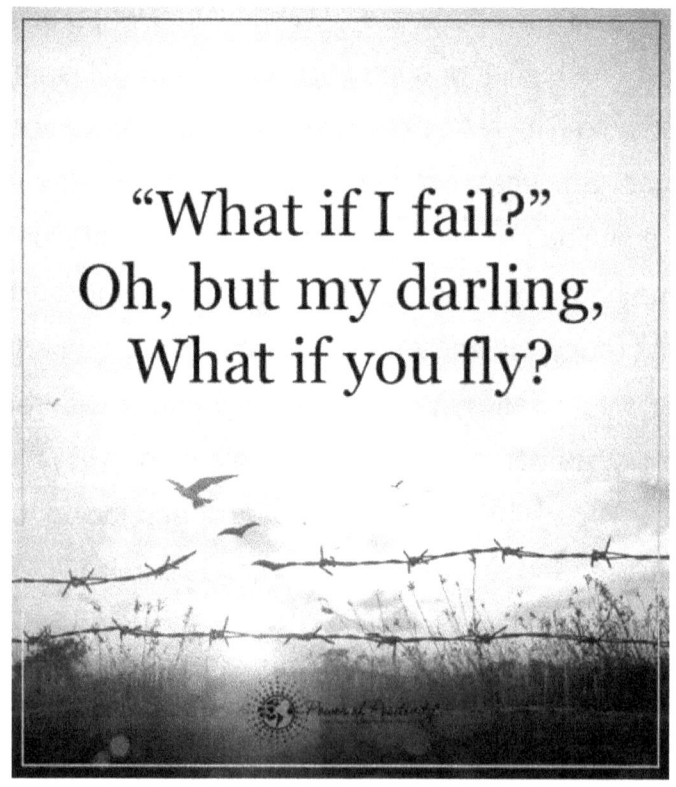

"Every major difficulty you face in life is a fork in the road. You choose which track you will head down, toward breakdown or breakthrough."

John Maxwell

Chapter 4

Working with Sellers

When I started my career in Real Estate, I mainly worked with buyers. Very quickly I realized that working with sellers was the name to the game. There are many reasons working with sellers is the name to the game.

I want to preface this by saying that Real Estate moves in waves. There are Buyers Markets, Sellers Markets and Neutral Markets. The shift from a Buyers Market to Sellers Market…or vice versa can happen very quickly. In fact, "shifts" happen quick. Shifts happen most of the time before anyone realizes there is a shift. When a shift happens, it may feel like a subtle shift but before you know it you are in a Full Fledge Buyer or Seller Market. If you work with Sellers and see we are transitioning into a buyer's market, you need to do 2 things. The first is to make sure the sellers are aware. Sometimes this is the hardest part because the seller doesn't realize the shift. Most times they may still think it is a Sellers Market. The media is slow to follow shifts.

When the media is saying the real estate market is "HOT" and you are a Savvy Real Estate Agent and realize the shift is coming or the shift has come it may be difficult to convince your seller that price matters or you may need a Price Reduction to stay ahead of the market. Keep in mind, the numbers don't lie. Sit down with your seller and show them market stats. Show them what is going on with New Listings On the Market, Average Days on Market, Expired Listings and Price Reductions.

Rule #1
Keep your pulse on the Market with market stats.

Rule # 2
Have those hard conversations with your sellers. Explain market shifts and show them the Numbers. The Numbers don't lie.

Rule # 3 - Make sure you start working with buyers. Get your strategy to incorporate buyers into your game plan (aka business plan) or else you will be twiddling your thumbs and waiting a lot longer for things to happen. With that being said, we will get into why "Working with Sellers" is the Name of the Game.

When I first started in Real Estate, I worked with a lot of buyers and a lot of investors. I didn't list property that much unless it was one of my investor's listings or the gazillion Short Sales I was working. I realized very quickly that Listings is the name of the game. Why? For a few reasons. First, you can handle more listings at one time than you can handle buyers. If done correctly and with the right team and system, you can handle 30 to 40 (if not more) listings at one time. Can you imagine working with 30 to 40 buyers at one time? It could never happen.

More listings mean more sales and more opportunities. Every listing, if marketed correctly, should bring you at least one buyer. With the sign in the yard and marketing the listing properly you should be able to generate more than 1 lead from each listing. When you are a Listing Agent, you work on YOUR time. Not someone else's. It is much easier to control your day and not let the day/ or a buyer control you. In this business, what do you think you are selling? If you answered "Yourself" you answered correct! You are in Sales. Sell yourself. That is what people are buying.

When you are a listing agent, you are selling yourself but you also have a product to sell. This allows for more marketing and outreach opportunities. Being a Listing Agent will allow you to maximize your time, money and energy. Would you like to go on vacation and sell real estate at the same time? Who wouldn't? You can do that when you are a listing agent. This is why I think that Listing Property is the name of the game!

Chapter 5

The Listing Presentation

So…you want to be a Listing Agent. Now What? In this Chapter I will discuss what to do on a Listing Presentation, what to include in the presentation and the rules when listing Property. Take out a pen and paper and take some notes or download the Working With Sellers guide in the Vault at www.realestatesecretsunlocked.com

Ask Yourself these questions:

Do you have a strong Listing Presentation or do you wing it every time?

Do you have the Objection Handlers memorized?

Do you have your Listing Presentation Memorized?

Do you Pre-Qualify Every Seller, Every Time?

Do you walk through the house with the seller the same way every time?

What is your Pre-Listing Routine?

What is your Post Listing Routine?

    If you don't have any of these, it is time to create your Listing Presentation. The best salespeople practice repetitious boredom. What that means is that if you want to be a strong listing agent. If you want to take a lot of listings. You have to do the same thing every time. This starts with the Pre-Qualification all the way through to taking the listing. You then need a Listing Plan once you take the listing that includes communication, showings, marketing, etc.

Pre-Qualifying the Seller

Pre-Qualifying the seller is one of the most important parts to the listing presentation. This is the first part in the process. This is where you decide to go on the appointment or not. Do not take listings from unmotivated sellers (unless they are in a high traffic area where you can put your sign and generate a lot of buyer leads). Unmotivated sellers cost you time, money and your peace of mind. There is nothing worse than getting calls week after week from the seller...wondering why their home won't sell, when you are holding the next Open House, and what you will do for marketing…. when you know they are WAY overpriced and not in a need to sell.

The Pre-Qualification Process should weed out the unmotivated sellers. The Pre-Qualification Process should also give you insight as to: what, why, where, when; What their plans are, why they are selling, where they are going and when they need to move by. You need to find out key facts. #1. Do they need to sell this home to buy something else? Why they are moving and what is their biggest "why," what is most important to them, where they are moving to and when do they need to be there? The "when" is very important. If they tell you they need to be moved within 3 months…then you better be reviewing their price and the average days on market. Sellers think they will put their home on the market and it will sell right away. It doesn't work like that. Let them know the Average Days on Market for a home like theirs to help them with the pricing and how long it should take to sell.

Pricing

Ask the seller what they think their home should sell for? What do they think they want to list the home at? This will help you determine the magnitude of the pricing objections you will be working with when you meet at the house.

Objections

The Pre-Qualification process will let you know UP-FRONT what their objections will be. NEVER handle objections over the Phone. Let them know that "_____ will be the very first thing you will discuss when we meet at your house"

FSBO/ EXPIRED

Find out if they are Considering a For Sale By Owner- if so, make sure you have your FSBO Objection Handlers. I have been in situations where I have gone on a Listing Appointment that was an Expired Listing, only to have them tell me at the dining room table that they will try For Sale By Owner. I was completely blindsided. Don't let that happen to you! Find out if they are considering going FSBO! That way you can explain the benefits of working with a strong listing agent like yourself!

Personality Style

One of the BEST Ways to build rapport is to give the seller exactly what they want. People like to do business with people like themselves. Determine their personality style and sell to them how they want to be sold to. If you are working with an Analytical person, bring market stats, graphs and numbers to satisfy them. Sell to them in their personality styles. If you are dealing with an Expressive, forget the graphs and stats. You will lose them within 5 minutes. Talk to them about how they feel. The emotional part of moving. Personality styles is THE MOST important part of the process. Make sure you learn your personality styles and learn to adapt to people. Remember, we have to Make them feel important. This is about THEM…NOT YOU! If you can become versatile, you will win more listings- hands down!

Motivation

You must DIG DEEP for motivation. Don't let THEM tell you their motivation. You decide! I have had sellers tell me they were not motivated, only to find out they were moving to Paris for a job transfer…and couldn't move until they sold their home. I have had a seller tell me she did not have to move, only to find out she could no longer do stairs and all the bedrooms were on the 2nd floor. The day of the listing presentation she had a hospital bed delivered for her downstairs living room because she could not make it up the stairs- still insisting that she was not motivated.

We have to help people make the best decisions for them. We also need to make sure we are working with motivated sellers so we do not take listings that we have no chance of selling. When you are Pre-Qualifying the seller, Ask questions that make them think. Ask questions and dig deep for motivation. You will then be able to use the answers to their questions again at the dining room table when they are giving you objections on Price, Motivation and Commission. Make sure you have your answers written!!!

Other Agents

Find out if they are interviewing other agents. If so, find out who…and when. This will allow you to see who you are going up against. Bring your stats. If you don't have any, bring your company Stats. If you are new, you can also ask a great listing agent in your office to go with you and if you get the listing, give a referral fee OR split the listing (but be careful!!! I have been burned in the past so make sure anything you do with another agent you have detailed information in writing). If you go on a Listing Presentation with another Realtor and you Split the Listing, you will want to make sure you have in writing what the commission split is, Who Does What for servicing the Listing and What Happens if the Listing Doesn't sell during the time you have it listed.

Confirm or Cancel

You decide to confirm or cancel the appointment. Remember, an unmotivated seller is not worth it. If the seller is WAY Over-Priced, not motivated or unrealistic then don't go. It is not worth it. Have the courage to cancel the appointment. There is nothing worse than taking a listing with an unmotivated seller and having the seller make unrealistic demands or call you week after week wondering why the home hasn't sold. You decide to Confirm or Cancel the appointment.

Check out the Vault at www.realestatesecretsunlocked.com for a copy of the Pre-Qualification Script.

Objection Handling on the Phone

Rule # 1

Never handle objections over the phone. That is the quickest way for the seller to cancel the appointment. At this point, on the phone you have little trust and rapport. Wait until you get to the home and go prepared! During the Pre-Qualification script you will ask them, "Do you have any questions before I arrive?" They may say, "What is your Commission," "How much do you charge," "I only want to take a 90 day listing," "What Price do you want to list it for," "I am not listing when you come out" and Blah…Blah… Blah…. Don't buy into it!!! This is a Reflex NO for them. Just like when you are walking into a store and you know you want to buy a Black Dress…. but when the salesperson asks you what you are looking for you say, "just browsing." It's the same thing.

What you need to say is "I understand _____ (commission) is important to you, and that is the very first thing we will cover when we meet on _____(Tuesday) at

_____(4pm)." Now…Listen!!! Don't freak out. Don't think you will go to the house and the moment you walk into the home they will drill you with the objections. That doesn't happen. You will go to the home, along with your Listing Presentation the way you normally do. They completely forgot you said that was the "first thing you would cover when you got there." It will probably come up at the end of the presentation but you will be prepared!!! You got this!!!

Another option for a phone objection: That's a Great Question and I am Glad You Asked! (I know _____ (commission) Is very important to you and that is one of the first things we will go over when we meet on ____ (Tuesday) at ___ (4) – Do you have any other questions?

Or,

I completely understand commission is important, and what I am hearing you say is that you want to Net the most Amount of Money from the Sale? (I agree!) That's Exactly why people like you hire me! (sound excited with an upbeat tone) and When we meet on _____ (Tuesday) at ____ (4pm) I will show you how commission can
be a tool to net you the most amount of $. That's what you want right? (Excellent!) Any other questions?

Objection Handling at the House:

Repeat, Approve, Affirm- Repeat their objection, Approve their objection (NEVER ARGUE!!! They are always "right"), Affirm what they are saying and then Handle the Objection.

What helped me with Objections at the "closing table" is that I always sent a Pre-Listing Package to the home or via email for their review. In the Pre-Listing package, I had the Sellers FAQ. The Sellers FAQ or Frequently Asked Questions had Every Objection and the answer to every Objection. I had this page "tabbed" and asked them to review prior to us getting together. This way they can review the objections and the answers before I got to the home. I can honestly tell you that this eliminated 90% of the objections I would get.

Objections

Remember when I said to Dig Deep for Motivation in the Pre-Qualification Script? This is when that comes into play. If someone tells you they want to only do a 5% commission, this is when you dig deep into their motivation and explain that the average agent sells 4 to 6 homes per year. If they only sell 4 to 6 homes per year, would you agree that they will show the homes where they get a full 3%

commission as opposed to only 2% or 2.5%? Then wouldn't you agree that to get maximum exposure for your home, we should list your home at the STANDARD 6% commission to get the most exposure and therefore getting you to _____ (Miami) by _____ (April)?

Here are my Top Rules for working with sellers:

Rule # 1- Work with Motivated Sellers- Unmotivated Sellers cost you Money and Time unless in a High Traffic Area (Sign)

Rule # 2 -Pre-Qualify Every Seller before going to the Listing Presentation

Rule # 3- Ask Essential Questions- Find out their motivation, the price they were thinking and if they are interviewing any other Real Estate Agents

Rule # 4- Have a Detailed CMA- Know the Neighborhood "Susy's House sold for Blah"

Rule # 5- Know your Market Stats (Average DOM- Set Expectations, Avg. Sales Price, Avg. Price per S.F.)

Rule # 6- Practice the objections (Objection is a Question in the mind of the buyer/seller- It's only an unanswered question. Don't get defensive)

Rule # 7- Show up on Time, Dressed Professionally and Ready to go!

Rule # 8- Determine their Personality Types during Pre-Qualification (Analytical/ Amiable/ Expressive/ Driver)

Rule # 9- Determine the Decision Maker- Sell to the Decision Maker

Rule # 10- MMFI- Don't Ramble on What you will do for them, Make this about them not you- Question Based Selling

Rule # 11- Question Based Selling and Tie Downs, NLP (Get them to yes) – Tom Hopkins, Matthew Ferry NLP, Mike Ferry

Listing Presentation Steps:

Step 1- Set Appointment and Pre-Qualify them
Step 2- Send Pre-Listing Package for them to review prior to appointment – you can Email it; Drop it off or direct them to your website

REAL ESTATE SECRETS UNLOCKED

Step 3- Show up dressed to impress, prepared and on time

Step 4- Walk through home with seller and build rapport – Take Notes and Go Three Deep! When building rapport, always ask Three Questions on the same subject. So, when you ask a question about them, follow it up with two more questions to get deeper into the conversation ABOUT THEM!!! Don't make it about you or bring "you" into it.

Step 5- Sit at the table and review their Pre-Qualification Questions (Why they are moving, what's important to them, timeframe, wants, needs, etc)

Step 6- Go over Listing Presentation/ Marketing Plan- emphasize what it is that every agent does, and what you will do differently

Step 7- Go over CMA and Pricing - Last

Step 8- Agree on Price and Sign the Contract

Step 9- Let them know when you will be back with lockbox and photos

Step 10- Servicing the listing

Now that we have outlined what TO DO in the Listing Presentation we will now cover what your listing presentation must include.

Your Listing Presentation must be either dropped off at the house OR sent via email PRIOR to going on the appointment. Why? What is the worst thing you hear when you have spent hours of preparing for the listing presentation, doing the CMA and going to the house for the presentation? After all of that.... what is the worst thing to hear the sellers say?!? You guessed it! "WE want to think it over."

When you send the Pre-Listing Package prior to the appointment, and the seller wants to "Think it over" you can then ask them "What specifically do you want to think about?" You can go over your listing presentation, marketing plan and stats and ask them What it is they want to think about. If you have not sent the Pre-Listing presentation to them prior to the appointment, it makes sense for them to want to "think about it" because they have not seen what you have to offer. If they want to "think it over" you then have only a 50% chance of getting the listings. So many things can happen. So, my suggestion is to send the Pre-Listing Package (with the Listing Agreement) prior to you going to the house. That way, they really don't have a lot to think over. So…. the question is, what do you have in your listing package?

You can check out my Listing Presentation in the Vault at www.realestatesecretsunlocked.com and feel free to copy!

I also want you to sit down and think about your listing presentation. What do you want it to include? What is important to you? What do you want the seller to know? What do you do for marketing? What do you do that differs from the 100s or 1000s of Real Estate Agents out there? What makes you…. you? You want to say to the Seller…This is what I do that EVERY OTHER REAL ESTATE AGENT does, and THIS IS WHAT I DO DIFFERENTLY.

Here are a Few Things your Listing Presentation MUST Include:

Bio

You have to have a Biography. About you. Think about what you bring to the table. You may be new to real estate, and that is OK! Maybe you have an eye for design, or are great at staging, offer free photography or are an excellent negotiator. Whatever you bring to the table you need to let them know. Take out a pad and pen. Write down all of your assets. What do you bring to the table? What sets you apart from all the other Real Estate Agents? Why should they pick you over the thousands of other agents in your area? What are your key attributes?

Plan of Action

What is your Plan of Action? What is your Marketing Plan? What are you going to do for Marketing, Showings, Photography, Staging if needed, Communication, etc? Take out a Pad and Pen. What can you do for FREE For the seller? Where does the MLS Syndicate to? Does it offer worldwide exposure? What does your company offer? Does your company have an international website to offer worldwide exposure? Do you offer Online Advertising, Facebook Ads, Open Houses, etc? What do you do for your sellers and your listings?

CMA

Have a completed CMA with 3 Active Listings and 3 Sold Listings Similar to the home in Square Footage, Bedrooms/Bathrooms, Pool/no pool/ Golf Course/ No Golf Course/ Water/ no Water/ etc. *** Keep In Mind---it DOES

NOT matter about the Active Listings as much as it matters what has sold. There may be listings that are Over- Priced. Make sure you point that out and show the seller what is actually SELLING. Your List Price should be based off of Sold Comps.

Market Stats

Market stats are probably one of the most important things to bring. If you can become an expert at explaining market stats (Especially to Analytical thinkers) then this will get people "back to earth" with Pricing and Price Reductions. You need to have the Average Days On Market (ADOM), Average and Median Active and Sold, Price Per Square Foot, Expired Listings and New on Market. You also MUST Have the Months of Inventory and explain Months of Inventory to the seller.

Keep in Mind….in an Appreciating Market you can list above the average sold price since prices are appreciating and still be OK….in a Depreciating Market, you MUST Price BELOW what the market is selling for (I would say 5%) because prices are going down and homes are sitting longer on the market. Make sure you become an Expert at market stats. This will allow you to move to any market and become an expert listing agent. Market stats don't lie!

You/Company Stats- Be prepared- You may get this question… How many homes have you sold in this neighborhood? If you haven't sold ANYTHING in the neighborhood, find out if your company has sold anything in the neighborhood. If So…always say "We just sold the home around the corner from you" Or "MY company has 3 listings in this neighborhood."

Pricing Pitfalls

Dangers of Overpricing – You must include the Dangers of Over Pricing. Sellers like to "List High" and then come down later…the problem with that is you might miss the market. In addition, what normally happens when you list a home and put a sign in the yard? Within a week or two…a few more signs go up. So, your Listing becomes the pricing median. Don't price high and come down later. The Pricing Pitfall Explanation should help you overcome that. If it doesn't…then you can always incorporate a Price Reduction in the Listing Agreement.

Frequently Asked Questions

This is a 100% MUST and has helped me overcome objections and WIN Listings. Make sure you have your "Seller FAQ" in your listing presentation. You can either come up with your own FAQ's or take mine from the Listing Presentation.

References

Have a list of references. Sellers you have worked with before. Buyers you have worked with before. If you are an Expired Listing agent or an FSBO Listing Agent (Like I was) make sure you have testimonials on how you have helped them sell their home when they were listed FSBO or Expired and it didn't sell…and how you were able to get it sold. Have a list of Expired of FSBO Listings, how long it was on the market prior to you and how long it took you to sell. Also include the List Price versus Sales Price Ratio.

Listing Presentation Marketing Plan

NOTE TO SELF…If the property is priced right, you will not have to do ½ of the things on your marketing plan. If you over-priced the property, this will cost you and your sellers time and money. Price the property right and it will sell!

At The Table

Sellers are clueless and probably haven't sold a home in years. You need to discuss the process with them from Signed Listing Agreement all the way to closing. Communication is key. You want to discuss how showings will be handled. Will you use a Lockbox or will it be Agent Accompanied Showings? If you are using a Lockbox, Bring one! Show them how it works and explain the benefit of the Lockbox system. If it is a Supra, show them how it works and that ONLY licensed agents can open it. You will know who goes in and out of the house with the Supra.

When I moved to Miami, the Real Estate Agents in Miami were SHOCKED that the sellers let me use a Lockbox on their homes. Apparently in Miami, it was Agent Accompanied Showings. That's what the Real Estate Agents were used to.

Here's the thing

When I moved from SW Florida to Miami, I came from an area where everyone uses a Lockbox (for the most part). In Miami, Lockboxes were NOT the Norm. In Miami, Agent Accompanied Showings were the norm or very common. When I moved to Miami, I got listings from Cold Calling expired listings and FSBO. My listings ranged from Homestead all the way up to Sunny Isles Beach. How on earth would I be able to take 15 to 20 listings (let alone 100's) and show each listing when I was working on a budget and didn't have money to hire a full time showing assistant? It wasn't going to happen. So, I explained the benefit of a lockbox to the seller at the Listing Presentation and guess what happened?!?! They all agreed that the Lockbox was the way to go.

    If you explain the process at the home during the listing presentation, you will want to share the benefits of your process and get "buy in" from the seller so you are all in agreement on how to handle showings. You will also want to go over the specifics of showings. Is there an alarm? Are there certain times you cannot show the home? Is there a gate or a doorman that you need to call for showings? Get the specifics so you know how to handle showings.

    I would use a Showing Service and let them handle the scheduling. Most MLS's provide a service. If you are going to do that, you need to let the seller know and explain how that works. You also need to discuss Open Houses. Some sellers love them and some hate them. Ask the seller how they feel about Open Houses. Do they want them? If they do, then who will do them? I can tell you my working hours were Monday through Friday. I wanted to spend the weekends with my family which meant I DID NOT do Open Houses.

    If the seller wanted an Open House, I would get someone from my office to sit them. Once in a while I would sit an Open House to satisfy the seller but for the most part I had another agent sit the Open House. However, what I did was call and/or door knock the entire neighborhood prior to the Open House to try to generate new listings or buyers.

Showing Feedback

I used a service for showing feedback. After the showings, It would email out a survey. The system I used also allowed the seller to get the feedback response. Don't allow it, and here is why. Let's say you have an overpriced listing, and you have been working on a price reduction because the home is NOT SELLING. The last thing you want to happen is to have an Inexperienced Agent show the home and comment on how the home is priced right. Then the seller sees that and the Price Reduction becomes an uphill battle. You need to monitor the feedback responses before it gets to the seller.

Remember, your number one goal is to HELP the Seller get their home sold. You must be strategic in how you do that. The sellers are emotionally invested in that home and the process. YOU ARE NOT. Keep them moving forward through the process.

Communication Guarantee

REAL ESTATE SECRETS UNLOCKED

The Number One complaint I heard all the time from sellers of expired listings was that the previous agent did not communicate with them. Always have a solution to every problem. Because I was so confident in my communication, I had a Communication Guarantee. My Communication Guarantee was that if they did not hear from me every week, they could fire me. That was written into the Listing Agreement under Additional Terms.

My system was that Every Friday I updated all my sellers. Pick a day of the week and update the sellers weekly. Give them the Showing Feedback, the amount of times the home was shown, the amount of times it was viewed on MLS, what you did to market the home that week AND update them on market stats. We need this more than ever in a shifting market or a Buyers Market. Let them know how many new homes came on the market and how many have sold. How many homes have expired off the market and what the inventory is. Let them know the day you will update them. This will eliminate the sellers calling you all the time asking for updates.

If you want to be a Listing Agent, you need a system. By having a system, you can then leverage. You can get other people to do the things you don't have time to do. Hire a Virtual Assistant to help with Marketing. My Virtual Assistant lives in the Philippines. I found her on Upwork and pay her $3.33 per hour. She is a rockstar when it comes to Marketing!!

At the Closing Table…

I can tell you I became the master at follow up after the appointment. Why? Because in the beginning… 80% of the time I left the home without a signed agreement. I can tell you that there is nothing more frustrating than spending time preparing for the appointment, doing your research for the CMA, getting to the home, doing the appointment, only to hear them say, "we want to think it over" or "we are interviewing a few more agents and then we will decide."

I had to fix this problem because I started to feel like a failure. Remember, ALL of my appointments were from cold calling. I didn't know these people. If it was a referral or if I knew them…then it was a lot easier. Anyway, I had to fix the issue of me not taking a listing right away…so what did I do? First, I got VERY GOOD at Pre-Qualifying the seller and making sure I was going on a solid Listing Appointment.

The second thing I did was find out who else they were interviewing so I can bring my stats or my companies stats to show how I compared to my competition. I also tried to strategically go on the appointment LAST and make them promise me they would sign nothing until they met with me. If all else failed, and I went on the appointment and they still wanted to think it over, even after I used every savvy objection handler to get them to say "YES" I then had to become a Bull Dog after the appointment.

How? The first thing was before I left the home, I scheduled another appointment to go back to the home to answer any additional questions. I would try to schedule that for the same week. I then called the sellers one hour after leaving the home and said "Thank you so much for meeting with me today. I am really excited to get your home on the market and I am confident I can get it sold. I know after leaving the home there may have been some questions that popped up so I just wanted to touch base with you and see if you had any other questions for me?" --- Try to get the Objections out of them and try to get them to move forward with signing the agreement. I would then send them a Thank You e-greeting the following day.

In this day and age, I would suggest sending them a Video Email or Text. You can use Bomb Bomb or just take a Video on your phone and text it to them. Thank them for the appointment and show them how aggressive you are with your follow up. I would stay on the seller like a bulldog until I got that agreement back. Sometimes it would take a few weeks, but I usually got the listing.

So, is this the way to take a Listing in an ideal world? NO! In an ideal world I would shimmy out of the home with my perfectly signed listing agreement, putting the lockbox on the door on my way out and calling the sign guy to put the sign in the yard. In a Not So Perfect world I would ride the seller for weeks and finally ending up with a listing agreement after exhausting them and exhausting me with my hard core follow up.

You are probably wondering how long you need to ride the seller for that agreement. If this is a saleable listing and they NEED to sell (not just WANT to sell), then you stay on them until you get the agreement or they list with another agent. Don't give up! You can never be too aggressive. You got this!!! Just work on getting better at getting a signed agreement at the table so you don't have to be an insane bulldog afterwards.

It takes daily practice to be good at your objection handlers at the table and getting them to YES. Remember, Real Estate is sales. YOU are in sales. You need to sell them on you. You need to sell them on listing the home and you need to sell them on price. So, practice your selling techniques. Practice your Objection handling. You got this! It takes daily practice and daily discipline. Find a Role Play Group or team up with someone in your office. Watch YouTube videos. Go to events like Mike Ferry, Tom Ferry and others. Become the Master at Objection Handling and you will not need to be a bulldog. You will shimmy right out of the home, jump in the car with a smile on your face feeling like "YOU DA BOSS" as you drive away.

Objection Handling- Here are a few tips when they are not wanting to sign:

Put Stipulations in the agreement.

If they tell you they want 24 hours to think it over then postdate the Listing agreement. Leave one for them and take one for you. Tell them you will rip up the agreement if they call you tomorrow and tell you they don't want to list the home with you. Let them know this will save them time as you will not have to come back out to the house. If they decide not to List, you will tear it up. If they decide to list then you will be able to get working on it right away. Also, they may tell you that Susy Q down the road said they were interested in buying. Well then put a stipulation that if Susy Q comes around In the next two weeks, you will not earn a commission OR you can represent them for a reduced commission (3%) and handle the transaction. Whatever their objections are, figure out how to solve it and put that stipulation in the agreement.

Never Argue

You never want to tell the seller they are wrong so you need to be very careful on how you word things. Always be on their side. You want to make them feel important. Always listen carefully to what they are saying.
Pricing- So the seller wants to list higher than you recommend. What do you do? Put a Price Reduction in the Listing Agreement. Have a stipulation that for the first two (or three) weeks you will price the home at their suggested price. If you do not get a lot of showings, then they agree to reduce the price to $_____.

Be Ok to Walk Away

Remember, you are in charge!!! If the seller has crazy ideas on showings, crazy expectations on what they think you should do to sell the home, crazy expectations on price, want you to sit an open house every weekend and will not allow other agents from the office to sit the open house, then be OK to WALK AWAY. Do not take a listing that you cannot sell or take a listing from an unrealistic seller. It is not worth it. You are better than that. There is nothing worse than looking at your phone only to see that crazy seller calling you for the umpteenth time in a day. Believe me, I have been there. It is better to spend your time finding another seller than dealing with the negativity and bad stigma from a crazy seller. When you walk into that Listing Agreement, Be OK to walk out of there without an agreement because it wasn't worth your time. Here's a Tip---let the seller know up-front that you may not take the listing. Ha! Use the old "takeaway" close and that may help you seal the deal!

Versatility

Remember, people like to do business with people that are just *Like Them*. Find out the personality style of your seller BEFORE going on the appointment, and become them when at the home. Bring them what they want. An Analytical wants stats, graphs and more stats and graphs. Bring them! An Expressive will fall asleep if you start going through graphs and stats, so leave them at home. See my notes on Versatility but remember, versatile selling is one of the most important things in this whole crazy game of selling. Become Versatile and you will win!

"Be a Chameleon. People Like Doing Business with People Like Themselves. Versatile Selling Will Win Every Time"

Danielle Damianov

Chapter 6

Lead Generation

Here is the thing. Yes, having a strong Listing Presentation is important. Yes, having a strong Buyer Presentation is important. Yes, knowing the market, the market stats, how to read a contract and every other thing that goes along with real estate is Important. However, none of that matters if you do not have any leads. None of that matters if you do not have any listing appointments to go on. None of that matters if you don't have any buyers to work with. None of that matters if you have no contracts to present or no one to share your market stats with.

So, the question is.... or should I say the loaded question is.... how do you find buyers and sellers? How do you get leads?

First, you need to ask yourself…how much money do you have to spend on Lead Generation? If the answer is a Big Fat ZERO (which was me when I got started) then you need to work for the business. If the answer is that you have money to buy leads, then you can BUY the business.

A lot of what I talk about in this chapter is about working for the business because that is what I had to do. I can tell you that there are a lot of very successful real estate agents out there that have a lot of money and can buy the business. However, the Return on Investment or the quicker way to get leads is to work for the business. Here is the thing. A lot of people don't want to work for the business because it's hard, it sucks, there is a ton of rejection and a lot of people don't want that. On the upside, there is a quicker return, more qualified buyers and sellers and it doesn't take as long. Once you get going, you will be able to do both (Work for the business and Buy the business) and will be able to grow and possibly double your business year after year.

Remember that chapter on Goals and your Why? This is where you are going to have a VERY strong Why. See, if your Why is not strong enough, then you will not keep going when that expired listing screams in your ear to never ever F***ing call him again (yes that has happened many times!) or when that old crabby lady slams the door in your face telling you "She will call you when she's ready and Don't Call or Stop By Again!" (yes, that has happened too!).

See, we will all experience rejection in this business. You may have a friend who bought a home from someone else or a family member list a home with someone else, or crabby frustrated people scream in your ear or your face. Remember, No Pain No Gain! We need to keep going. Your Why will keep you going. Lead Generation is NOT FUN! NO ONE likes it, but if we don't do it we will be looking for a second job or getting out of the business altogether.

We have to remember. Real Estate is a Sales Business. A lot of people do not look at it like a Sales Business, but it is. Not only is it a Sales Business, we are selling one of the most important assets in a lot of people's lives. For some people, the equity in their home is their life savings, their kids' College Fund, their Retirement. So, we need to make sure we understand that and we protect one of their most important assets.

In addition, we need to remember that since we are in sales. We need to generate leads. We need to find buyers and sellers on a daily basis in order to protect our income, our kids' college savings, our retirement and our future. This is our business. Are you all in? If so, remember your Why. That will keep you going. That will keep you motivated. That will be why you do what you do. Even if it means calling Expired listings 3 hours a day, 5 days a week looking for buyers and sellers. Even if it means Door knocking Pre-Foreclosures to see how you can help with their short sales. Even if it means calling personal representatives for Probate to see how you can help. Remember, this is your job. Finding people who need to buy and sell real estate. You are coming from a place of contribution. You are helping them. At the same time, you are providing a life and a future for your family and if you work this business right, you are providing a Great Life for yourself.

Again, focus on our Why. If your children are your Why and your goal is to have them attend private school, then how many deals do you have to do in order to pay for the school? That results in how many contacts/appointments/etc. you have to do/have to reach your goal.

"When that nasty lady hangs up on me, I look at my kids' faces on the goal board and I keep going." Prospecting is the direct link/connection between your Why and your goals…You need to make your Why so big that failure is not an option. Keep it in front of you.

Remember:

The Bigger your Why, the Bigger your Goals, the more Leads you have to Generate.

The Bigger your Why, the Bigger your Goals, the tighter schedule you have to follow.

The Bigger your Why, the Bigger your Goals, the better you need to be at Pre-Qualifying your Leads – If you Generate you don't have to Tolerate.

The Bigger Your Why, the Bigger your Goals, the better you have to be at Lead Follow Up – Remember Leads will Bring You Leads – Lead Follow Up will bring you $$$.

Things to Think About

Get a Pen and Paper, or write in your Journal or this book and Ask Yourself:

What are you currently doing for Lead Generation? List all of the sources you currently get your leads from.

Does your Company Give you Leads? If so, what percentage of your leads are Self-Sourced and What are Company Driven?

If you are 100% Company Driven, Ask yourself what would happen if you ever wanted to leave your company or your team? Where would your leads come from?

Do you have a Lead Generation System that CONSISTENTLY generates leads on a Daily Basis?

Are you on a Roller Coaster? Do you get really busy with your "leads" or "clients" and are on top of the Roller Coaster---only to Stop Generating Leads and find your clients either don't Sell or you lose a deal and then you are on the bottom of the Roller Coaster ---with No Leads, No Deals and No Clients?

Are you Being Re-Active with your Day or Pro-Active with your Day?

Are you Consistently out there looking for Business? Are your antennas up at a Restaurant, at the Daycare or the Soccer Field, listening to People say they want to Buy or Sell real estate?

What is the 1 Thing that if you do it Every Workday (5 days a week) That can increase or dramatically increase your Business?

Do you Start your Day with Daily Lead Generating?

So now that you have reflected on what you currently have going on, let's add some Active and Passive Lead Generation to your day so you can make some more money!!!

I am going to Review some Different Passive and Active Lead Generation ideas. Pick the ONE Thing from each category that you can:

Add to your Daily Routine
Do it 5 days a week Consistently
Have the Resources to Do it
Make sure it fits with your Daily Schedule and your Lifestyle

Passive Lead Generation

Passive Lead Generation are things that may or may not bring you immediate business AND it can be hard to track your Return on Investment. When using Passive Lead Generation Techniques, you need to be in it for the long haul. It takes time. It doesn't happen overnight and it takes patience. Here are some Passive Lead Generation ideas:

Social Media

In this Day and Age, you need to be on Social Media. Especially if you are looking to GROW your business. I know there are some "old schoolers" out there killing it that may not have a Facebook page or any other Social Media Platforms …BUT…if you are new or looking to grow, Social Media is a

MUST. You need to have a mix of both Personal and Business on your Facebook page.

When I first started out I was so secretive. I didn't want to have my personal life exploited. I didn't want everyone to see my personal life. I can tell you that the moment I started revealing more of "me" and more of my family...my business picked up. People want to know more about you. This is a People business. We need to connect with people. If you don't want people to see more about your personal life and/or are not on Social Media...then this is not for you!

Newsletters

Be the Area Expert!!! In this day and age, I would suggest posting a video for a Monthly or Weekly Newsletter. Do NOT have it be all about Real Estate. You need to engage with people that are not looking for real estate at this moment. If you can engage with them even if they are not interested in Real Estate, with informational things to keep their attention, hopefully they will reach out to you when they are interested or when they hear someone that is.

Mailers

Mailers are postcards or newsletters to your audience or possible FSBO's, Expireds, etc. Here's the thing about mailers. They take a lot of time and cost money. If you don't have a lot of money for at least 12 months of mailers, don't use this technique. You need to create a brand and get your name out there. Most mailers end up in the garbage unless you hit the jackpot and find someone needing to sell and they have no idea what Real Estate Agent to use. I have spent a lot of money on mailers with very little return.

However, when I was farming an area and trying to become the neighborhood expert (which I did!!), I did a Quarterly Newsletter and sent it out to the neighborhood with local neighborhood news, tips, the market stats and my personal stats in the neighborhood; that did get me listings. That being said, mailers can cost quite a bit of money and you need to be in for the long haul or it doesn't make sense to start it in the first place.

Online Leads

Buying leads can work. BUT it can also cost a lot of money. A lot of online lead generation providers such as Zillow, Commissions Inc, Boomtown, etc. can cost a lot of money and the return on investment can be very slow. I know a lot of agents who are spending thousands of dollars a month and not seeing a return. They say it's a long term investment. Is it worth it for you? I don't know. You will need to ask yourself how much money you have and if you can sustain it for 12 months or longer with little return?

Facebook Ads

I can say that Facebook Ads do work. I have seen firsthand that Facebook Ads can definitely bring you business. What I have also seen is that people that try to do their own Facebook ads (unless it's your thing and you are computer savvy) it doesn't work. It is best to hire a social media consultant and have them do the Facebook ads for you. Have a budget and hire someone else to do this for you. You should be selling homes, not doing Facebook ads.

Networking

Networking is great but you need to make sure you are networking with people that can bring you business. You also have to network the "right" way. You cannot walk into a networking event and give everyone a spiel about you. The way to get people to like you is to ask people about themselves. People like to talk about themselves. So, ask them about them, their business, their life, their interests. At networking events, make it about the person you are talking to. Not about you.

Get their business card (I pretend I forgot mine so I can get theirs and I can then follow up with an email and email them my contact information). There is a book called "Networking is not Working." Read it!!! It is a great book that gives insight on networking. Keep in mind that networking is another long term play. Don't expect to go to a networking event and get business immediately. It doesn't work like that. You need to foster the relationships and give back. I would give and not expect anything. Eventually you will start to receive more than you know. Make sure to put the business cards you receive into your CRM and send them something of value.

Advertising

I have seen the craziest advertisements out there. I remember walking through a grocery store and seeing a Real Estate Agent on the grocery store cart. Now who is really going to go to a grocery store and write down the Real Estate Agent information on the cart? Maybe there is someone, but to be honest with you…I don't get it. You can advertise on billboards, bus benches, magazines, and church bulletins, for example. I have advertised in a variety of these places and have seen no return. Remember, in a lot of markets…everyone knows a Real Estate Agent. So, what is the likelihood that you will call a stranger that you see on a shopping cart over a Real Estate Agent that you know or that is referred to you?

Open Houses

So many Real Estate Agents sit Open Houses but how many Real Estate Agents make a killing from this activity? Not many. Look at the Top Listing Agents in your market. Do you ever see them sitting an Open House? Probably not. Now, they may have other Real Estate Agents from their office sitting an Open House but rarely will you see a Top Dog sitting an Open House. As you are starting out in your career, and if you don't have weekend plans, then this activity may get you out in the community, meeting people, getting to know the market and inventory.

Now don't be one of "those Real Estate Agents" (like me..LOL!) that feels weird making people sign in. Remember, this is your job. Make sure you get the contact information for everyone coming to the open house so you can put them in your CRM and follow up. At the very least they should be in your CRM getting something of value (do not bombard with market stats). If you don't get people's contact information and if you don't ask them a series of questions while they are looking around the house then what is the point of sitting the Open House?

      In regard to Marketing, a lot of Real Estate Agents (me included) have an Open House, drive there 10 minutes before, put out a few signs and sit. If you are sitting an Open House this is the perfect time to actively look for Buyers and Sellers. Door Knock the neighborhood a few days before. Invite all the neighbors for a 1 hour neighbor preview before the Open House. Bring flyers to pass out to the neighbors and ask them who they know that might be looking to move into their neighborhood, and then follow up with "Have you considered moving?"

      You may even want to preface it with something about the market, like "Rates are really great right now" or "Right now is an amazing time to Buy and Sell." The other thing you will want to do is call the area a few days before letting them know about the area and using the same script. Now when you are calling, your whole goal is to find other people to buy and sell real estate. It's not really to let people know about the Open House. Even if this is NOT your listing, you still want to do this activity. Remember, Your job is to find people that need your services. Sitting an Open House gives you an opportunity to let the world know you have something to sell and it also gives you the opportunity to see who else needs you.

      You want to also make sure you blast it on Social Media, Facebook, Instagram, all the Real Estate Websites and you can also do a Facebook Live at the house that day showing everything the house has to offer. You may want to also team up with your favorite Mortgage Professional or Title Company to help you market. If you work every Open House this way you will be on your way to being one of the Top Real Estate Agents in your area. If you work the Open House by flying to the house a few minutes before, throwing out a few signs and twiddling your thumbs wondering why no one showed up while contemplating getting a second job as a Walmart Greeter, then your road to the top is going to be a lot slower and you may be getting a new job or a new career before you ever see the top.

Online Reviews

      This is HUGE. You need to be asking for Online Reviews on Google, Yelp, Zillow, Realtor.com and everywhere people can find you online. There are some companies out there like Social Survey or Testimonial Tree and others where you can get reviews. There is no better feeling than to say to a buyer or seller "just Google me" and up pop several different reviews (all Five Star!!) about your service. If you are not getting reviews currently, make it part of your practice that after every deal you send out a Thank You email or a survey (Survey Monkey), asking about your business and asking for a review.

Cause Marketing

If you haven't heard the term Cause Marketing, you likely have experienced companies that offer Cause Marketing. Think of the brand TOMS. Did you know that for every pair of shoes you buy, they will give a pair of shoes to someone in need?

So, what is your cause? Think about it. Come up with something that is important to you. My grandmother died from Alzheimers and Mental Illness has run in my family so the National Association of Mental Illness is an important cause for me. On every listing appointment, I would tell my seller that, after closing, a portion of my commission would go to a charity of their choice. If they did not have a preference, then I would donate to the National Association of Mental Illness.

You can do something like that OR if you have causes that are very important to you such as Pets for Vets, Fostering Animals, Homelessness, Big Brothers Big Sisters, etc., make that part of your marketing. Let everyone know what your cause is. Some people will want to do business with you because they believe in the same cause. Cause Marketing is a Passive Marketing Technique and it can also be used for branding yourself and aligning yourself with a cause that is important to you. This will also allow you to network, get involved with the organization and it will get you out there meeting people. That is what you need. To meet people and find out who is looking to buy and sell!! Remember, everything you do must be intentional if you want to make it big or make it at all in this business.

Video

If you are not doing videos you need to start. Video has been around for a while now. More people watch videos over reading. You need to keep your videos short and sweet. Try to keep them under 3 minutes and get straight to the point. There are so many things you can do with video. I suggest you get a YouTube Channel to host all of your videos. You can do videos about the process, Why Listings Expire, Why FSBO's Eventually List with an Agent, What is Title Insurance, etc.

You can Interview your local attorney, your home inspector and everyone in your "network." Those are all informational videos that you can refer your prospects to, AND look like the area expert. Remember though, you don't want to be "all Real Estate" or else people will get bored and not want to watch you unless they are in the market to buy or sell. So, you need to do some exciting videos.

Check into making videos like "New Hot Restaurants" and interview the chef or the manager. Or, do a video on the "Hot New Communities," by showing the features and benefits of each community. If you are a golfer, interview the golf pros in golfing communities nearby and show the features of the golf courses. Do video tours of the beaches, the ski resorts, the neighborhoods, and anything and everything about your area. You can also do a monthly video of the Market Stats and a weekly video of your "Listing of the week." Get out there and start shooting. Our cell phones have made it so easy to do quick videos and upload them to various sites. You can also use services like Bomb Bomb or Vyral Marketing.

Out of the Box Thinking

There are so many new ways to advertise now that the church bulletin is not going to cut it. You can advertise on Podcasts, Instagram, Waze, Alexa, Pandora and so many other online resources. Check out the advertising costs for these different advertising mediums. How cool would it be if someone is listening to Pandora and all of a sudden your ad came up? Or they are driving down the street using Waze to get around and all of a sudden they see your ad and your office pop up on the screen. Make sure they know very quickly what you do and how to reach you.

Facebook, Craigslist and Online – How many times do we advertise an Open House or our individual listings? What if you don't have an individual listing or an Open House to Advertise? Instead of advertising ONE thing, start to advertise so it will appeal to a much larger audience. For example, advertising a List of Foreclosed Properties in your area. Advertise Pool Homes under $350,000 in your area. Advertise a list of Off-Market Properties (i.e.. FSBO's), advertise a List of Waterfront Homes between $300,000 to $600,000. Start to figure out your ideal client, make sure there is turn over in that market and advertise a List of Homes instead of just one home (an open house or your listing). You can put these ads on Craigslist, Facebook, Instagram and so many other mediums. This can also be your ad on Pandora, Alexa, Podcasts, etc.

Figure out what will appeal to more people and advertise "THAT!" You can also add the 1-800- Home Info to the ad, so people can call an 800 Number for a recording, that way they don't feel pressured. The cool thing about the 800 Number is there is no obligation and no pressure on their end

BUT you immediately get notified that they have called that number AND you get their contact information so you can follow-up with them.

Active Lead Generating

As I sit here writing this book, I am on a flight from Fort Myers, Florida to Boston, Massachusetts. What's interesting is that when my Uber driver pulled up to my house to bring me to the airport, he had a huge door Magnet on his car for his Real Estate Business. Now don't get me wrong, there is nothing wrong with working a second job. But typically, people in Real Estate get a second job, or get out of the business because they are not cutting it in Real Estate. That being said, they still would rather drive strangers around all day in their car putting on miles and miles for pennies, instead of taking two hours a day, five days a week doing something they most likely Hate, but that would make them a ton of money.

Think about it. Would you rather spend 10 hours a week, prospecting for new business with the return of a six or seven figure income, or would you rather spend 6, 8, 10 hours a day driving random people around to make a few thousand dollars?

I know that Active Lead Generating is hard. I know it is not fun. I know you will get screamed at, told to F***K Off, hung up on, etc. BUT there are people that need you. There are people that need your services. It's a numbers game and you just have to find the right ones. I can tell you that my business was made from calling expired listings. That's what I did. Five days a week, 3 hours per day and 30 contacts a day. Was it fun? No. Did it eventually become 2nd nature? Yes.

It also allowed me to work five days a week, no weekends, on my own schedule, on MY time and make six figures. One of my biggest and craziest weaknesses is that I would rather call Expired Listings and For Sale By Owners than call my database, past clients and sphere of influence. To this day, I still have clients that I have worked with 7 or 8 years ago calling me and telling me about their life, their travels, etc. This job can be very hard, yet it is so rewarding.

According to The National Association of Real Estate Agents (NAR) 2019 Profile of Home Buyers and Sellers (https://www.nar.Real Estate Agent/infographics/2019-profile-of-home-buyers-sellers) the Statistics say that 41% of Buyers and 66% of Sellers found their agent through a referral from a friend, a neighbor or relative OR they used an agent that they worked with before to buy or sell a home. So, my thought is, referrals cost you nothing! You just need a good system to stay in touch with your past clients and sphere. Call them and ask them for the business.

Please take note: You MUST do Active Lead Generating Daily to generate new business. But if you want to get to the top fast, do not make the same mistake I did. Get a System where you Consistently call the people you know and call the people you don't know. If you have a system, where after a deal closes your clients go into a Database and you routinely call them once a quarter, your business will skyrocket.

It's funny because I talk to so many Real Estate Agents and ask them where their business comes from. The Real Estate Agents that tell me Referrals, never do any cold calling and the Real Estate Agents that tell me cold calling, never call their database. Why is that? I have no idea but I can tell you I probably would have a lot more money than I do today if I had a system where I regularly called my database; if I had a system where I regularly called my past clients. Do not just put your clients in your CRM and drip on them with real estate newsletters. That does not work. You need to CALL them. Yes, pick up the phone and CALL them.

Now, you can put them in your CRM, send them something of value, send them cards (I like Postable), and send them text messages (I like Textingbase.com) but you also need to check in quarterly. See how they are doing AND ask them who they know that might be thinking of buying or selling real estate. Real Estate Agents get most of their business from Referrals and Past Clients…this is a no brainer.

But for the Real Estate Agents, like myself, calling our past clients and sphere is downright scary!!! For some reason, I never wanted to feel like I was begging for business or didn't want to come off as desperate. That was my thing. If I called Expireds or FSBO's, I knew they needed my help and they needed it fast. That is no excuse for me not calling my database. I just had to change my mindset to realize my past clients and database had people that needed my help too. I also had to realize that this is my business. This is how I fed my family. This is how I lived and my family needed me to call.

So, the bottom line is that Active Lead Generating is not fun. It can be hard. You won't want to do it. BUT, it is a MUST if you want to be a top Real Estate Agent, make a lot of money and NOT have to become and Uber Driver or Walmart Greeter just to make ends meet. So, here are my tips and ideas for Active Lead Generating.

Expired Listings

I loved expired listings. Why? Because you know they most likely want or need to sell. They are willing to pay a commission. They are probably frustrated because their home didn't sell. They might be more realistic on price. My statistics for selling Expired Listings was almost 100%, meaning that I very rarely had a listing expire. Why? Because if I went on an Expired Listing appointment and it was over-priced and the seller wouldn't budge, I walked away and didn't take the listing. If the seller was unreasonable on showings or the house was a wreck, I walked away. I would not take a non-saleable listing. The other reason is because I was very good at communication. I would communicate the market; the market stats and I was very good at price reductions.

So why do listings expire? Usually it is because the house looks like $#IT on the MLS. The Real Estate Agents got a Listing and took shitty pictures with their cell phone, pictures are upside down, toilet seats are up, beds are not made and so many other things. Do you really think someone is going to fall in love with a house online if the pictures look like crap? I had a Professional Photographer and a Virtual Tour regardless if I had a $100,000 condo to sell or a $2 Million dollar listings. Professional Photos are a MUST!!!

The second issue is that Real Estate Agents do the 3 P's, which is Put a sign in the Yard, Put it on the MLS and Pray it sells. Now that might work in a seller's market, but that will NOT work in a balanced or a buyers market. You have to watch your listings. You need to see how many showings you have. How many people are looking at it online and NOT coming to see it. Where are the comparable homes priced in comparison and you MUST communicate this to your seller in a way they understand.

The number one complaint I got from expired listing sellers was that their Real Estate Agent did not communicate with them. So, I became the MASTER of communication. So much so that I had a clause in my Listing Agreement, as I mentioned already, that if for any reason they felt I was not communicating with them on the terms we have set forward they could fire me immediately. I was confident in my communication. I knew it would never be an issue and I also knew my 3% was at stake if I failed. Communication is key!

How to Prospect Expireds

First of all, I hear Real Estate Agents tell me that they call expireds once or twice a week. If you are going to call expireds once or twice a week, don't do it at all. Why? You are up against the bulldog Real Estate Agents of Expireds. They call Daily. They know their scripts. They don't take "NO" for an answer. In fact, they know that the first "NO" is always a Reflex. When you call Expireds you cannot take the first "no" as a "NO." In the beginning I fell for it. In the beginning I would never get any appointments and then wonder why I would see them listed on the MLS a few days later. I was frustrated and broke.

When I learned that no matter what the Expireds say, you need to keep asking questions to find out the What, Why, Where, and When. Then you can really determine their motivation. Remember, you determine their motivation. Not them. You need to take them down the sales funnel to help them get what they want, and that is to sell their house.

Calling Expireds

You must call them daily, five days a week. You must call more than once. You need a dialer. Hand dialing Expireds is not going to work. I also suggest a three-line dialer so you are taking more turns at bat and able to talk to more people. Do not research the expired listing before calling. Just call. My schedule was to wake up every day, Monday through Friday. I would role play from 7:30 to 8am and then hit the phones calling expireds at 8am. Real Estate Agents always ask if 8am is too early. The answer is NO.

Do you know how many other Real Estate Agents are calling at 8am or in some instances 7:45am? You want to be one of the first few to call. If you are the 10th, or 15th you probably don't have a chance. They will be mad and extremely frustrated by the time you call, even if you are calling them at 9am. I also suggest that once you go through the new Expireds, you call the other expireds that you missed the days and weeks before and then the even older expireds. Don't stop calling; get into the habit of calling them daily. Know your scripts and your objection handlers. Practice them daily. Calling Expired Listings can be the key from going from good to great or to go from NO business to a listing machine.

The best thing about calling expireds is that once you get good, you can move markets and still be a listing machine. I moved from SW Florida to Miami and had business within 30 days from calling Expireds. If you are good, you can go on vacation and schedule two hours per day to call expireds from wherever you are and send a teammate to go on the listing appointments and split the listing. There are so many opportunities with expireds. Is it fun? No! Is it challenging? Yes! Does it take time to master? Yes! But this source is by far, in my opinion, one of the best sources to drum up immediate business and become a listing machine.

For Sale By Owners (FSBOs)

This is another great source to take new listings and it can be a little easier to find their information. You can find them on websites like fsbo.com, byowner.com, Craigslist, Facebook, Nextdoor and the local newspaper. The good thing about FSBO's is that most of the time they want to sell. What they are trying to do is save money. What they don't realize is that you will save them so much more money by hiring you. This is the most important thing you need to share with them.

A lot of FSBO's will try it on their own with the intention of listing it with a Real Estate Agent within a month or two if it doesn't sell. You need to find them, call them and then set yourself up with a weekly "touch" to stay top of mind, while asking for a Listing Appointment to show them how you will save them money. My line used to be "If I can show you how I can Net you the Same amount of Money, if not More, by using me as your Real Estate Agent….would that be worth 15 minutes of your time? (Hint: Wait for them to speak and the answer is usually "Yes" …or "How are you going to do that?") Then I would say "That's exactly why we need to together, so I can show you how I can Net you the Same amount of Money if not more. What works better for you, I can meet you today at _____ or tomorrow at _____?" You always want to go for the appointment.

So, you might be thinking, how CAN I net them the same amount of money if not more? Here are some reasons why.

Getting an Offer on a home is the easy part. Going from Contract to Close is when the real work happens. I have seen so many people lose thousands of dollars because they didn't follow the contract or didn't know how to properly negotiate after a low appraisal, or a bad home inspection. You are the expert at negotiating and can save them thousands. In addition, you know your way around the contracts and will not let them lose any money.

Listing with you, you offer them worldwide exposure through your Marketing Campaigns. More exposure means more buyers and more opportunities to make the most amount of money on the sale.

Professional Photography

Pictures sell. If you are not using professional photography... you need to start. Professional photography enhances the chance the home will sell for Top Dollar.

Statistics

Show them statistics from the National Association of Real Estate Agents that shows how much more money home sellers got from Agent Assisted Sales than Buy-Owner Sales. You can also find an article online (I had this in my toolbox) that shows the owner of www.forsalebyowner.com listed his home with a Real Estate Agent.

Prospecting

If you are a prospector than you are always actively looking for buyers and sellers. You can tell them you take a Pro-Active approach to finding buyers for your listings by Door Knocking the neighborhood or calling the neighborhood. If they are in a gated community, ask for the Community Directory. This is one of the best ways to get in touch with the neighbors to see who they know that is looking to buy a home.

Strategically Priced

You are an expert on Price. You know how to price property for it to sell.

Typically, FSBOs will pay 3% to the buyers agent. They are just trying to save the additional 3%. You must show them how you are able to net them the additional 3% that they are trying to save.

Just Listed/ Just Sold

This is probably one of the easier calls to make. When we first moved to Miami from SW Florida I did not have any listings. I called Expireds and For Sale By Owners every morning. I would then get my hands on a listing that my company had and call around that listing and make the Just Listed or Just Sold calls. My very first listing in Miami came from the Just Listed call. If you do not have any listings, you can ask another agent at your company to call around their listing. Technically you don't have to ask but I always did.

I would find a listing in an area that I wanted to work and then call around the listing and say "Hi, My name is Danielle with EWM Realty and my company just listed a gorgeous home right around the corner from you. It has ____ Bedrooms and ____ Bathrooms and it is listed at $ _____. I'm just curious, who do you know that would like to move into the area?" You can find scripts for these calls online. You want to keep it simple, keep it fun and always ask them if they have considered selling their home. The goal is to get listings. If they showed interest in the home or was asking questions about it, I would ask them for their email address so I can send them the virtual tour. Here are some tips for these types of calls.

Don't call them too early. These are not Expireds. I would suggest calling them mid-morning. You can also call them in the afternoon once they are getting home from work.

Use a service like Coles Realty Service to get their phone numbers. You can also ask for the neighborhood directory if they are in a gated community.

Door Knocking works too! If you want to door knock, you can door knock the neighborhood and bring flyers. I would suggest keeping a copy of your script on a clipboard. You have to make sure you are asking who they know that is looking to buy/sell and if they have considered selling.

Set a Goal

You want to have a goal of how many people you are going to talk to so that you don't get chatting up the lonely old neighbor and never make it to the other houses. Believe me, that can happen! I suggest having a contact goal and a lead goal. How many contacts are you going to make and how many leads are you going to get? Don't stop until you reach it. That will keep you focused!!

Probate

So, I am going to be honest. Probate was one of the areas I was starting to break into when I was living in Miami. Why? I wanted to move my business from a strict prospecting based business to a referral based business. My thought was to go the Probate Route and become a Probate Specialist. I went and got my Certified Probate Real Estate Specialist designation with MTI Education. They send you all the material for the Self-Study course and have lots of different tools to help you. I put my designations on all my social media sites. I created a Probate Page on my website with helpful information for the Personal Representatives.

The thing about probate is that most of the time the families want to sell the home or need to sell the home in order to settle the estate. The personal representative is the one in charge and a lot of times they have no idea what they are doing. They need your help. The homes may be in disarray. They need someone that has a team of people to assist. This person is you! As a Probate Real Estate Specialist, you have your team of people if you needed to coordinate an Estate Sale, a Handyman or General Contractor, Title, Attorney, etc. You are their go-to person for all of the real estate needs. Once you identify yourself as an expert in the probate field or a specialist in the probate field then you can go out and get business. Here are the steps I took.

Connect with Estate and Probate Attorneys on LinkedIn. Let them know that you are a Certified Probate Residential Specialist (CPRES) and invite them to meet for coffee. At the appointment, ask them about their business and how you can help. Typically, what they need is a CMA because when they are dealing with the estate they need to have an idea what the property is worth. Let them know you offer free CMA's and find out other ways you can help them.

Estate and Guardianship Committees

I am not sure if they have this everywhere but in Miami there was a monthly "lunch and learn" for the Estate and Guardianship Committees. You did not have to be an Attorney to attend but all the Probate and Guardianship attorneys and judges were there. This was a great way to get out and network with these attorneys. I highly suggest that you see if there is one in your area. Host a lunch and learn for the group. Attend their meetings and outings. Get involved and get your name out there!

Coffee/Lunch

Most of the attorneys eat at the same restaurants by the courthouse. If you are meeting an attorney for coffee or lunch I suggest you meet them at their favorite spot by the courthouse. Chances are they will bump into other attorneys that they know and hopefully make an introduction. This worked for me!

Probate Data

This is not in every area so you need to check and see if they have the service in your area. This company pulls the probate information and will give you the contact information for the Personal Representative. They will also give you the data for the Attorney. You can work this two ways. The first is by calling the Personal Representative. This conversation is not always a good one. You need to let them know you are calling to help and find out what their plans are with the Estate. You have the tools to help them on your website (which you can get from MTI Education) and to show them the probate process. Calling the Personal Representative of the Estate is not always the easiest call to make but this is how you can get straight to the source. The second way you can work this is by emailing the attorney. I always put the case number in the Subject Line and believe it or not, the attorneys usually emailed or called me back. You can find out what the plans are with the Estate and if they need a CPRES Real Estate Agent to help. Again, you might also want to ask the attorney to coffee or lunch.

REAL ESTATE SECRETS UNLOCKED

Short Sales

Back in 2008 when Short Sales were rampant and I needed to work my butt off, I pulled the Lis Pendens every day from the Clerk of Court website and I would door knock them. Within a few months I had 30 listings from Short Sales. The thing about Short Sales is that people need help. They don't know how to deal with the bank. They are not going to beat you up on Price because they don't care, they just want the house sold. Right now, it is July 2019 and I am seeing short sales making a comeback and I think we are going to see more and more of that in the next two to three years. I suggest going after short sale listings because a lot of people are not doing that. You can find a Short Sale Negotiator to negotiate the short sales for you. Just focus on taking the listings and getting them sold.

Tenant Occupied Properties

So, here is the thing. If a home is on the MLS for sale and there is a Tenant in the Property, the Tenant more than likely needs to find a new home. In today's market rents are high. The tenant has to pay first, last and security deposit on a new rental home. They can more than likely buy a home for the same amount of money it would cost them to rent a home and their mortgage payment might even be cheaper. Reach out to the tenant in Tenant Occupied Homes for sale. Preview the property or send them a letter. Turn the tenant into a buyer!!

Landlords and Evictions

In many states Evictions are Public Records. You can have a Virtual Assistant pull the Eviction Notices and reach out to the landlord. The Landlord is more than likely fed up with his investment and may want to sell.

Estate Sales

Hit up the yard sales and estate sales on Saturday and Sunday. A lot of time homeowners will hold an estate sale before getting the home on the market to sell. Go to the yard sales and estate sales and talk to the homeowners. Find out if they are thinking of selling.

Senior Market

I loved working with the Senior Market. I found that they did need more help and there have been many times where I would have to help organize an estate sale or get a handyman over to the home to get it picture perfect. You can get your SRES designations which is the Senior Real Estate Specialist. I suggest going to the nursing homes in the area and ask about holding an informational seminar on taking the next step in life. You can have all different vendors and affiliates and a panel of people to discuss what they need to do if they are thinking about downsizing to a smaller place or even a nursing home.

Relocation

If you live in an area with major companies I suggest you get in touch with HR and figure out how to become a Relocation Specialist. Get on their list! Help people moving into the area or out of the area for work purposes. Become the Go To Real Estate Agent for all their Relocation needs!

Divorce

Typically, when people get divorced they either need to refinance their home or sell their home. You can work the divorce market the same way you work the probate market. Get in good with the divorce attorneys in your area. Take them to lunch or coffee. Go to their meetings and events.

Schmooze them until you become their Go To Real Estate Agent!

Seminars

Team up with other affiliates like a Mortgage Broker, Title Company, Insurance Agent and Home Inspector and hold a seminar. You can hold these at the Local Library, a Community Clubhouse, a Restaurant, Conference Rooms, Total Wine, etc. Hold a First Time Home Buyer Seminar to target people currently renting and are thinking of buying, or hold a VA Seminar for the veterans in the area, or a Senior Housing Seminar for seniors looking to downsize or move to a Retirement Community. Seminars are the way to go.

The challenge with the seminars is marketing and getting butts in seats. So, you need to be strategic. Figure out what your budget is, get other Affiliates to pitch in and spend two months marketing your seminar before you hold the seminar. Most Real Estate Agents worry about what they are going to say or how they are going to present the material but that is not the challenge. The challenge is getting people to attend. Don't worry about your presentation until you know you have enough people attending and that you are going to continue to host the seminar. Spend your time worrying about the marketing for attendance before you worry about the presentation. I've had to cancel many seminars because we didn't spend the time focusing on attendance and getting as many people there as possible, and our turnout was going to be low so it didn't make sense to continue with the seminar. Spend more time and energy on filling up the seminar to make sure you will have a good turnout.

Real Estate Agents in Other Markets

Living in Miami we had a ton of people moving from New York City. Part of my prospecting routine was to reach out to other Real Estate Agents in NYC and let them know that I am a local real estate agent and I pay a 25% Referral Fee. This got me business! Where do you have people moving from? Reach out to other Real Estate Agents on Facebook/ LinkedIn/ Email and let them know you are a full-time agent and you pay a 25% referral fee for any clients they have moving into your area.

Virtual Assistants

In the beginning you need to do the work yourself so you can figure out exactly how you are going to approach your prospecting. Once you have it down, I suggest you hire a Virtual Assistant to do it for you. I always made my cold calls daily from 8 to 11 (1. Expired 2. FSBO 3. JL / JS). When it came to Probate and Referrals I had my Virtual Assistant message the attorneys daily and schedule coffee/lunch appointments; she also messaged Real Estate Agents in NYC letting them know I pay referrals. You can also have your Virtual Assistant pull the numbers for you, pull the Lis Pendens, pull Eviction Notices, schedule coffee and lunch appointments and so much more! I used Upwork.com for my Virtual Assistant and would definitely recommend it, but there are several other sites as well.

    Active Lead Generating is the most important job you have as a Real Estate Agent. The issue is that most Real Estate Agents do not do any Active Lead Generating. They are a Secret Agent that does Passive Lead Generating that only generates enough business for them to barely survive. If you want to have a Massive Real Estate Business or a Business that allows you to travel, take exotic vacations, drive a nice car, put the kids through college, retire with a nice retirement, then Active Lead Generating must be done daily and 80% of your day must be spent doing this.

    I hate to break it to you, but as I've mentioned (with expired listings, for example) this must be done in the morning because if you plan to do it in the afternoon, most of the time you won't get to it. Active Lead Generating is not always fun but it is necessary to have a good business. How big your business is will depend on how effectively and efficiently and consistently you do Active Lead Generating on a daily basis. Bottom line!

Resources for Lead Generation

Vulcan 7, ARCHAgent, Redex, Landvoice and Mojo- These are all services to get you phone numbers for Expired Listings and For Sale By Owners and some of them come with their own dialer

Coles Realty Resources- This will give you neighborhood phone numbers that can be used for circle prospecting, Just Listed/ Just Sold calls

MailChimp, Constant Contact- These are services that you can use to send out Customizable Newsletter; they also act as CRMs!

Referral Services – Referral Services are where you can sign up for a service and pay a fee to that company to receive Leads. Below are just a few:

Dave Ramsey- ELP
Agent Machine/Referral Exchange

DANIELLE DAMIANOV

Zillow/ Trulia/ Real Estate Agent.com

As I reflect on my days as a Real Estate Agent, I remind myself that sales is sales and regardless if you are a Real Estate Agent, Mortgage Broker, Car Salesman, Boat Salesman, Restaurant Equipment Salesman, etc…. sales is sales and these Top Three Things are what I constantly had to remind myself:

I Must Get better and Stronger at Pre-Qualifying My Leads. How frustrating is it to spend time chasing a lead that never turns into a deal? How frustrating is it to spend time chasing a lead that buys through someone else? If I am stronger in my Pre-Qualification, I will be able to determine who is really going to buy and who is not. Keep in mind...Motivations and Needs change, so even if you pre-qualify them up-front you need to continuously ask pre-qualifying questions. Things change in people's lives. They may be serious buyers now only to find out a few weeks into the home search that they are moving cross country for a job change. You have to consistently ask pre-qualifying questions to make sure their motivation or need is still there.

Consistently Call My Database. This is the one thing I always struggled with. For some reason I would rather pick up the phone and call Expired Listings and FSBO's daily then call the people that know, like and trust me or people that I have done business with in the past. If I consistently called my database I probably would have doubled my business. This one thing can take you from Good to Great. Don't neglect your database. Call them Consistently. Make sure you Ask for Business. Find out who they know that might be looking to buy, sell, invest or build. Don't ignore your database. They want you to call them!!!!

      Master Lead Follow Up. Here is the thing. Most people are not buying or taking the bait on the first call. Keep in mind that leads…bring you Leads. Lead follow up brings you Money!!!! The Money is in the follow up. You have to be a Master at lead follow up. The challenge can be getting a system to regularly call your leads. You must have a system to call your leads. You must put your leads into a system so that they are not on pieces of paper that you can lose. For Referral leads, I use Pipedrive. It is cheap and a great way to track your leads, keep them in one place, track the leads you "win" or "lose" and you can access this on your Phone or Computer. Remember: The Money is in the lead follow up, so ask yourself:

What System do you currently have to follow up on your leads?

How often do you follow up on your leads?

How many deals have you lost due to bad lead follow up (and if you say none then you are not talking to enough people or you don't have enough leads)?

What system or Plan are you going to do to Master your Lead Follow Up?

The Roller Coaster! I know we have all been on the Roller Coaster of the Real Estate Cycle. The Roller Coaster can bring Great Highs and Great Lows. I can tell you my Roller Coaster always went like this: in the low of the roller coaster I am freaking out. I have no deals or very little deals pending, I am not getting a lot of leads, I start to get scared so I focus like crazy on prospecting, determining what leads I need to follow up on to get people off the fence and things start to improve. Now I am going up the hill and everything is great. I am working my butt off on Lead Generation, Prospecting, Marketing and it is all coming together. I now have deals…lots of deals…lots of prospects…lots of appointments and I feel amazing!!! The problem is now I feel overwhelmed. I cannot let these deals die, I cannot have bad customer service and I can't do it all so I STOP my Lead Generation and crazy prospecting to focus on the deals I have going on.

This part is fun! I like focusing on the deals. I love working with buyers and sellers BUT these deals start closing or some may fall through and die. I haven't been keeping up with my consistent prospecting because in my mind, I cannot handle any more deals anyways…but now what happens? The deals either die or close and I am back on the bottom of the roller coaster with No Deals, No Prospects and No Leads. Why? Because I stopped doing the ONE THING That got me all of the deals and leads. Don't Do It!!! Don't Be Like Me! This was one of my Biggest Mistakes. Do Not Stop your Lead Generation because of Overwhelm.

If you do not have enough money to hire a transaction coordinator or an assistant than find another Real Estate Agent in your office that you like and trust to help you with your deals and give them a referral fee. Maybe it is a rookie Real Estate Agent that wants to learn and is willing to do or handle your deals the way you want them handled, or maybe it's an experienced agent that will work the deal with you 50/50. Whatever you do, do not stop your Lead Generation or you will constantly be back on that roller coaster and I can tell you, those Lows are not fun. They are scary. It all goes back to your Why. If your Why isn't big enough, it won't motivate or push you to keep going. Keep your Goals in front of you. Remind yourself daily what your Goals are. Keep going, keep pushing and you will be Unstoppable!

DANIELLE DAMIANOV

PLAN – The Top Agents PLAN Daily:
        Prospect
        Lead Follow up
        Appointments – Buyers and Sellers
        Negotiate Contracts

PLANP- The New Agents MUST PLANP Daily:
        Prospect
        Lead Follow Up
        Appointments- Buyer and Sellers
        Negotiate Contracts
        Preview Property

PPP- The Inexperienced Agents do PPP
        Put Home on MLS
        Put a Sign in the Yard
        Pray It Sells

Chapter 7

Working with Buyers

When you get started in Real Estate, I think the majority of newbie Real Estate Agents get started working with buyers. Buyers seems like the easy transition into Real Estate. The thing is, buyers can suck the life out of you. Buyers can have you running all over town for months only to "cheat on you" and buy from another agent. You have to make sure you are working your buyers the right way or they will leave you feeling defeated, rejected and going crazy. So, let's start off with the Rules on Working with buyers.

Rule # 1 – Only Work with Committed Buyers. If a Buyer is not willing to commit to you and work with you, then do not waste your time. There is nothing worse than spending months or even years working with a buyer only to find out they had no intention of buying or were not in a position to buy. Get their Buy-In and get them to Commit to you!

Rule #2- Call them immediately and stay in touch. If you get a call from a buyer or a referral- you must call them immediately and have a solid follow up plan to stay in touch with them. If you are not using a Buyer Broker Agreement, then it can be stressful. You never know if they will cheat on you and buy from someone else. Lead follow up and a solid communication plan is imperative when working with buyers.

Rule # 3- Prequalify your Buyers for Motivation – 100% of the time. You do not want to be a tour guide. You need to make sure you are working with serious and committed buyers. How do you know if your buyers are serious and motivated? You find out through the Pre Qualifying process. You must have a series of questions that you ask the buyers to determine their timeframe for buying, the amount they are prequalified for, if they are serious and ready to buy and if there are any conditions of the purchase (i.e.. if they need to sell their home first, a job transfer, etc).

Rule # 4- Have a Buyer Presentation and explain the process- trust me...Buyers do not get it. Most buyers only buy a home once every 5 to 7 years or longer. They forget how it works and if they are not in Sales, they don't realize that you only get paid if you sell them a home. When you sit down and have a Buyer Presentation with them, you will explain the process. We will talk more about the Buyer Presentation in this chapter but this is an Imperative step when working with buyers.

Rule # 5- Have your Buyers Pre-Qualified for a Mortgage or have Proof of Funds Ready if they are paying cash. This must be done 100% of the time. As a Mortgage Broker, I can tell you that I have worked with Real Estate Agents that have spent months with a buyer...only to find out that they were looking at homes WAY above what the buyer was pre-qualified for...or even worse, the buyer was not qualified at all. You do not want to waste your time working with a buyer and showing them homes that they cannot afford. You must have your buyers pre-qualified 100% of the time or it is not worth spending time showing them homes.

Rule # 6- Set Standards – You must set standards with your buyers. I remember talking to a Real Estate Agent who was spending days showing rentals. In our market, a rental only pays $300 to $500 and the rentals they were looking at was an hour from his home. Why would you spend your days working and showing rentals to only make a few hundred dollars? There are Real Estate Agents that will travel one…two…three hours outside of their markets to show property. Why? In my opinion, it is better to refer that out and get a referral fee and spend my time finding more buyers or sellers than wasting time going outside of my market. Think about the standards you want to create for yourself and here are a few questions to ask yourself:

Do I have a Minimum Sales Price I want to work with?

If I have a buyer that wants to look at Rentals, will I work it or refer that out?

What is the timeframe for a buyer that I will work with---if a buyer is not going to buy for a year or more, how much time will I spend with them?

If a buyer will not get pre-qualified before starting the process, will I work with them?

Do I have a radius that I work with my buyers, and how far outside of my market will I go?

Standards are important and standards will keep you on track. I know that we all get sidetracked, we all get excited when we have a potential deal, but if we work every possibility that comes our way we will find out really quick that we are spinning our wheels and spending more time with buyers that are not going to do anything. We must have standards in our business so that we can make sure we are working with ready, able and willing buyers and if we are not, then we must spend more time finding the right buyers that are ready, able and willing to buy. The busier you get, the higher your standards need to be.

Buyer Presentation- The Benefits

If you were going on a Listing Presentation, chances are you will have a Listing Presentation to bring with you on the appointment that outlines what you are going to do for the seller and what you will do to get the property sold. The funny thing is that most Real Estate Agents do not have a Buyer Presentation. Why? The Buyer Presentation is equally as important and sometimes more important than a Listing Presentation. This will separate you from the competition. This will allow you to determine if these buyers are worth YOUR Time. Here are the Benefits of the Buyer Presentation.

Benefit # 1

You will quickly find out if the buyers are motivated or not. If the buyer will not go through a Buyer Presentation with you whether it is on Skype/ Zoom, On the Phone or in the Office than they are not worth your time. The Buyer Presentation will allow you to find out if they are motivated or not, their timeframe for buying, if they are pre-qualified or need to get pre-qualified, if they are working with any other agents and most importantly exactly what they are looking for.

Benefit # 2

When you do your Buyer Presentation, you will do your Wants and Needs Analysis. You will be able to help them figure out exactly what they are looking for, what they want and what they need, their location and price point. By really Digging Deep in the Buyer Presentation, this will allow you to narrow down your home search. This will also allow you to match properties to your buyers based upon their wants/needs. If you are constantly sending your buyers properties or showing your buyers properties that do not fit their criteria, they are going to get annoyed and start to think that you don't know what you are doing. It is important to take the time upfront to really figure out what they are looking for so you can send them homes they are interested in.

Benefit # 3

Separate yourself from the Competition. You see, the thing is that most Real Estate Agents will get a call from a buyer to go see "123 Main Street"…so what do they do? They jump in the car and go show "123 Main street" with no objective, no idea if they qualify for "123 Main street" and no questions asked. By having an in-depth Buyer Presentation, you are able to separate yourself from the competition and this will allow you to build Rapport with your buyers. Buyers …people, for that matter…want and like to talk about themselves. When you are having a Buyer Presentation and really listen to what it is they are looking for, this will allow you to build rapport with your clients and will help solidify a commitment for them working with you.

Benefit # 4

Open Houses/ Builders and FSBO's- One of the biggest reasons we get scared when working with a buyer is because we know that if we have our kids birthday party on a

Sunday...and have a motivated buyer with no Buyer Broker Agreement signed, there is a chance that they can swing into an Open House on your one day off and make an offer...without you...and you have now just spent months with them only to get cut out of your hard earned commission because you had to take a day off. You see, with the Buyer Presentation, you are going to talk to your Buyers and explain the process. Explain to them what to do when they go to an Open House, a For Sale By Owner or a Builder. Explain how you get paid, how the process works and give them a stack of your cards in case they stop by an Open House, For Sale By Owner or Builder. If you do not have a Buyer Presentation, then you run the risk of working long days and nights for free because your buyer cheated and bought through someone else.

Buyer Presentation- What it Includes:

Why You.

You don't want to have a lengthy buyer presentation or people won't read it. However, you do need a good 1 page Bio About You. Don't have the Bio be all business. Talk about you. What you enjoy doing, about your family, your kids, your passions, what charities you are involved with or community involvement. What are your passions. Have you done any leadership involvement, etc.? You also want to tie that in with how you help people buy and sell homes. What are your strengths, what designations you have and include why working with you will benefit the Buyer. Include what separates you for the Competition (AKA Other Real Estate Agents). If you are struggling with coming up with things that separates you, here are a few to think of, and ones that I used.

You Find Off-Market Properties

Now you might be thinking that you don't really find off-market properties...but can you? The answer is yes. What people don't understand is that not every single listing in the MLS makes it to Zillow, Realtor.com and all of those other sites that syndicate to the MLS. I know that certain Real Estate Boards have you check a box that says if you want the listings on those other sites. Not every Seller wants their home Public on Zillow, Realtor.com, etc. In addition, if you have a Buyer that is looking for a certain home in a certain area and you are not finding it, you can let everyone know in your Real Estate office and organization what your buyers are looking for. You can also circle prospect the area they are looking in and call and/or door knock homes with your buyers specific needs and find out who is looking to sell. Your Job is to find them the perfect home and you will go above and beyond to make that happen. Now THAT is why they should HIRE YOU instead of your competition. When they hire you, you go to work to find them the perfect home and facilitate the sale. Your service is free for them except maybe a transaction fee.

Strong Negotiator

As I talked about a little earlier, I always told my Buyers and Sellers that getting a contract on a home is the easy part. Getting from Contract to Close is the hard part. There are so many intricacies in a contract. If a Buyer does not know their way around a contract they can lose thousands, or even hundreds of thousands of dollars, depending on how much money they have in escrow.

The first part of negotiating is the price. This can be tricky so you need to know how to read comps (Comparable Sales). The last thing you want to do is have your buyer pay more for a property than it is worth. The next negotiations can come after the Home Inspection, Appraisal, Mortgage Commitment Contingency. You may have to Re-Negotiate if there are issues in the Home Inspection. You may have to Re-Negotiate if there are issues with a Low Appraisal. You may have to Re-Negotiate if you do not have a Mortgage Commitment and your contingency is close to being up.

All of these timelines in a contract are real. If you miss one, your buyer can lose their escrow. It is important to let your buyers know that not only do you know your way around your contracts but you are an expert negotiator when it comes to protecting your buyers hard earned money. If you do not have the CNE Designation (Certified Negotiation Expert) I would suggest looking into it.

Your Team

Introduce your team! In the buyer process, there are a team of people that work on getting from Contract to Close. Most people do not buy a home very often. If they are not in the business, chances are they do not know or have a Home Inspector, Handyman, Escrow Agent, Real Estate Attorney, Title Company, Insurance Agent, Home Warranty Company…and the list goes on. So, who is on your team? If you do not have a team, you need to invest some time in creating one. I never like to recommend someone that I don't trust.

When I moved to Miami, even though I was not new to the business I was new to the area so I didn't have a team. What I did was talk to the Real Estate Agents at my company (if your company is small, you can look at Real Estate Agents in your Real Estate Board) especially to the ones I looked up to, that I respected and that did a lot of business. I knew their reputation was important to them so I trusted their opinion. I would find out who they used for Home Inspections, Septic Inspections, Insurance Agents, Mortgage Brokers, Handymen, Attorneys, etc. Once you have your team, you will include the list in your Buyer Presentation. I know some people would say to recommend at least three people, however, that can confuse them. If I have someone I really like working with and feel comfortable with them, I would recommend just them. If there was a personality conflict I would then recommend someone else.

      You can even take "Your Team" a step further. I used to call myself a "Lifestyle Specialist." I am also what I would call "a Connector." I love making recommendations for everything from great restaurants, my favorite hair stylist, etc. Since I live in Florida and have lived in the Tampa/St. Pete area, Naples/Fort Myers area and Miami area, I always worked with a lot of people new to the area. They were looking for good restaurants, good places to shop, good stylists, the best beaches, etc. My team consisted of people that will get the job done and then I would have a page of recommendations.

You can also take this ANOTHER STEP further and create a mini coupon book for your favorite places and include home cleaning companies, power wash services, painting, restaurants, etc, that you hand to your buyers at closing. Not only will you be promoting your favorite local restaurants and local places to shop, but they may in turn refer you to their friends and family when they hear of someone looking to buy or sell. This idea is something I have had for a while and never implemented the coupon book but I think it is a great idea.

Now that I am in Mortgage, I can do the same thing. It would be a great closing gift and will allow you to spread the word and gives you a great reason to reach out to your "team" and ask them who they know that is looking to buy or sell real estate! If you do your coupon book, Please Share on our Facebook Group Called Realtors Guide to Mass Production and let us know how you are doing and who you've included in your Coupon Book!!

Communities

If you are in an Area like SWFL you have hundreds of Golf Communities, Boating Communities, etc. It is important when working with a Buyer that you know your communities. For example, if you are working with a Boater and they are looking in Cape Coral, Florida…. Cape Coral, Florida has hundreds of canals. In fact, we have heard that they compare Cape Coral to the Venice, Italy of the United States because of the canals. The thing is, some canals are freshwater and some are not. Some have direct access to the open waters of the Caloosahatchee River or the Gulf of Mexico and some have no way out or many bridges to get out. Some canals are just minutes to the open water and some may take hours. The last thing you want to do when working with a Buyer that has a sailboat, for example, is to show them, OR WORSE sell them a home that does not have sailboat access to the open water.

      In addition, if you are Working with a buyer in a Golf Course Community, you need to know the Association Fees, what they include, does it have bundled golf or non-bundled golf. All of this can be confusing. You need to relay this information to your buyers and Show them that when they work for you, you will find out all the information prior to showing properties to make sure you are matching the right properties with the right buyers. You must explain this to them so that they don't go Rogue and start hitting up all the Weekend Open Houses or FSBO's and cut you out of the deal.

Part Two- Explain the Process

So, we have all heard the term, "Buyers are Liars"- but are they? I think that sometimes they can be liars, but most of the time the problem is that they don't understand how real estate works. Most of the buyers you work with are not in sales. Most of them buy and sell a home once every 5, 10 or 20 years. They forget how it works. It is your job, during the Buyer Presentation to explain the process. You should have a Step By Step chart in your Buyer Presentation but you also need to verbally explain the following:

Your service: What it includes and what it will cost them.

Most Buyer Agents get paid by the Seller or the Builder. If they get charged anything it may be a transaction fee at closing, so your service is basically free for them. They need to know this but they ALSO need to know that you do not get paid unless you sell them a home. You need to explain that you are on Straight Commission and if they decide to go around you and go straight to the Builder, FSBO or Real Estate Agent at the Open House that you will not get anything. You want to hand them a Stack of your Cards and tell them that if they do stop by an Open House, FSBO or a New Construction Community to let the agents know that they are working with you. Let them know that you will negotiate on their behalf and that you will work for them to negotiate the best deal and guide them through the transaction. This is so important to have this conversation!

Understanding your Buyers and their Wants and Needs analysis.

Sitting down and having the Wants and Needs Analysis is so important! This is where you are going to find out exactly what your buyer is looking for. There is nothing worse than spending weeks or months with a buyer showing property and never finding the right thing. If you start showing them too many homes and you are constantly not showing them the "right" homes they are going to start losing confidence. They may then start to go off on their own, or worse, find a different agent. You need to make sure you take the time to find out exactly what it is they are looking for. Why they are moving. What their Motivation is. What their Time Frame is. What is important to them about their new home.

You may want to give your buyers a Questionnaire before you even meet with them. That way when you get together you are reviewing the answers to the questions and will be able to dig deep. I would suggest creating a PDF that they can print or a Fillable PDF and also create an online version. You can go to Survey Monkey and create a "survey" that they fill in. I think that creating a Survey Monkey is the best idea. You will want to send the survey to all parties involved in the buying process. If you are working with a couple, send them each one. They will have different ideas on what they are looking for. You will then want to compare the similarities and differences in the Questionnaire they completed and discuss it at the meeting. You want to find out what is the Most Important thing to them and what can they "go without." What do they love about their current home and what do they not like? Here are a few questions to include in your list.

    What is the Most Important to you about your new home? (Size, Square footage, Bedrooms, Bathrooms, Pool/No Pool, Etc.) Take it a step further. If they say they absolutely need 4 bedrooms, find out why. If they have three kids and each want their own room, then don't show them less than 4 beds. If they are a retired couple and have a home office, find out if a 3 bedroom plus a den would work. Dig deep to find out exactly what they want and why. I had a buyer that was looking in Coral Gables. We spent almost a year and were not able to find what they were looking for. Once we opened up our area to Coconut Grove, they immediately fell in love with the home and bought it. They are still there 6 years later! If only I knew that Coconut Grove was an option...maybe I would have found them their new home sooner. Make sure you ask questions to really find out what they are looking for.

Timeframe

When are they looking to buy? Do they want to move or do they HAVE to move? If they HAVE To Move, what is the Drop Dead Date. Do they have to sell a home prior to moving? If so, explain how a simultaneous closing can work. Most people cannot figure out the logistics. You are here to make the transition as seamless as possible. What has to happen in order for them to be able to buy and what is the timeframe for buying?

Location

What Location are they looking in? Do they want to be in a specific school district, in a specific community, do they need to be close to work, what is their lifestyle...do they want a Boating Community, Golf Community, close to Shopping and Restaurants or a Rural Lifestyle; do they want to be on the Waterfront or close to the Beach, close to a Ski Resort, etc.? What is the maximum amount of drive time to

Work/School/Shops/Restaurants, etc. Dig deep to find the location and what is important to them.

Price Range

What is the Minimum and Maximum Price they can go? Have they spoken to a Mortgage Broker? Most Buyers don't realize that an additional $25,000 in price does not make a whole hell of a difference in their monthly mortgage payment BUT it may make a HUGE Difference in what they can buy. Make sure they talk to a Mortgage Professional to see what they qualify for and if they don't have one, they can call me! My contact information is in the back of this book and I will be more than happy to go over it with them. You can also get my Mortgage Application and Download it to your cell phone to help determine how much they can afford at www.lendfla.com and join the Real Estate Agents Guide to Mass Production Facebook Group.

Financing or Cash

If they are getting a Mortgage, they must get pre-approved before you take them out looking. Here is the thing, in this business time is money. I have worked both sides of the business (Real Estate and Mortgage). There are many people that have NO CLUE what their financial position is to buy a home. They don't know how income is calculated. They may not realize that Self-Employed borrowers can have issues with buying a home due to how their income reports on their taxes. The last thing you want to do is spend days, weeks or months with a buyer only to find out they don't qualify for a home.

      If they are getting a Mortgage you must make them get Pre-Qualified first. Life can get in the way so ask your buyer if you are able to give your favorite lender their contact information so the lender can reach out. If they are paying cash, let them know that you will need to include their Proof of Funds with the offer or a letter from their banker or financial advisor that they have the funds to buy the home.

Personality Styles – this is so important to figure out!! Now you are not going to put this as a question on the questionnaire but I want you to sharpen your skills and start to understand people's personality styles. People like to work with people that are exactly like themselves. We've talked about this before, but this is just a reminder that If you are dealing with an Analytical Personality Style, you need to bring them stats and figures so they can analyze the numbers. If you are dealing with an Expressive, they will get bored with stats and figures and will go by how they feel; the last thing you will want to do is bring an expressive pages and pages of stats and figures. When you are having the meeting, get a feel for their personality and show them properties and sell to them in their style (not yours!!!) This will help you build rapport.

Ask for the Agreement

Now I am going to be completely honest with you, I asked for my buyers to Sign a Buyer Broker agreement maybe 10% of the time. I don't know why. I think I was scared or it wasn't the "Norm" in my market so I just didn't do it. Now, that being said...if I were to go back in time and become a Real Estate Agent and do it all over again I would get REALLY GOOD at my Buyer Presentation and would ask for the Commitment 100% of the time. Why? Because I hated the feeling of working with a buyer and knowing that any time they can walk into an Open House, or a FSBO, or a Builder and cut me out of the deal.

I have a family and would sacrifice my weekends and evenings showing property, having to miss out on family events or having to pay a babysitter to watch my kids when I knew there was the possibility that they would go with another agent. Think about it, would the way you run your business change if you worked with buyers that had a buyer broker agreement? Would you run the business on your time instead of theirs if you knew that they are committed to you? I think the answer would be yes. If you work with a lot of buyers, I would suggest starting to incorporate the Buyer Broker Agreement into your Buyer Presentation. Get really good with it and Work on your "Objection Handlers". I would also recommend having a "Communication Commitment" where if you are not communicating with them, they will be allowed to fire you. This may make them feel more comfortable with signing it.

A Buyer Broker Agreement is a Great Idea. When working with Sellers, you have a listing agreement. So why don't we have one when working with buyers? Especially since Buyers take up much more of our time. I would incorporate this in my Buyer Presentation and make it a goal to get one signed when working with buyers!!! If you currently get a Buyer Broker Agreement signed, please share it in our Community on Facebook at "Realtors Guide to Mass Production." I love videos so a video example of how you use it in your business would be amazing!!!

Showing Property

If you start showing buyers a ton of properties and nothing interests them you need to go back to the Buyer Questionnaire. Sometimes when buyers start to see properties they realize that what they initially wanted has changed. Check in with your buyers. Re-group and go over the questions again. See if what they initially wanted is still what they actually do want. Is there anything that they have seen that they actually Like or Don't Like or is no longer a Priority or is now a Must Have? The last thing you want to do is spend days, weeks, months or a year (yes I have worked with a buyer for over a year) and get them frustrated. If that happens they may think you are not listening to them or cannot find them what they want, so they go elsewhere. Having a Strong Buyer Presentation and a Strong Wants and Needs Analysis should eliminate this. That being said, here are the Rules for Showing Property:

Don't show a lot of properties in one day. It can confuse them. Now I completely understand if you are in a destination market that you will have buyers flying into town with only two or three days to look at properties. In that case, if they are in town, and ready to buy a home, you may have to spend two to three days showing property…all…day….long. If they buy, it's worth it. If they don't buy, you just spent days of your time not knowing if they will eventually buy or not. So, if that is the case…ask yourself if it is worth it and what you can do differently next time. Are they not looking to buy for another year? If so, could you have referred that buyer out?

If you have ready, serious and able buyers, take your time doing the Wants and Needs Questionnaire, and Dig Deep for what they really want; show them 3 to 5 homes in one day that meet all their qualifications and then at the end of the day, ask if they are ready to make an offer on any of the homes you have shown them. A good up-front consultation will eliminate the homes they will not like.

Do not bring a ton of information on each property. I made the mistake in the beginning of giving them all of the information on the property the moment they got to the home. So, what did they end up doing? They spent the time at the home shuffling through the paperwork instead of really looking at the home. Take your time at the home and give them information on the home AFTER you do your walk through so they can review it later.

Take notes!!! As you walk through the home with the buyers, take notes on what they like and don't like. Some Real Estate Agents like to let the buyers walk through the home by themselves. I liked to give them their space BUT, at the same time, I liked to hear what they like and don't like. That way I can help them remember their likes and dislikes for each home. Have a clipboard. Have the Home Detail Sheet that highlights all of the important features of the home (ie. Taxes, HOA Dues, Size of the Lot, the Size of the Home, Upgrades, etc.). Then on the back of the Detail Sheet, take notes of what they like and dislike. After each showing, spend 5 minutes discussing the home and take notes! That way you can start to get a feel for what they are really looking for.

Preview Property. If you have buyers looking for a specific property it is so important to take time to preview property. If you are in a market where Broker Opens are the norm, go to them. Spend that day looking at all the homes available for sale. If you are not in a market where Broker Opens are the norm…go to Open Houses. This will not only allow you to match buyers with properties and properties with buyers, but it will also allow you to get to know your market and what is for sale.

Always be a student. See what other Real Estate Agents are doing. How are they marketing? Is it working? What do you like and what do you not like and adapt it to your own style. When you begin to preview property you now have a good reason to call your buyers back and let them know what is out there on the market. By doing this activity I sold a Million Dollar Home in Coconut Grove to my buyer that only wanted Coral Gables. When I saw this home at a Broker Open, I knew it was the right home for them. I called them immediately and asked them to stop over to view the home. We had an offer drafted that night. When you find properties for your buyers that they would have never found on their own, you are the hero! It gives the most satisfaction. Go out there, preview properties and become an expert in your market!!!

Making the Offer

Listing Agents list homes based on comps but sometimes based on what the client wants or what the client needs to net. Now…if I was the listing agent, I would never list above Market Value UNLESS we were in an appreciating market. Not everyone is like that. If you are working with a buyer and they fall in love with a home in their price point but the home is way above Market Value, you need to know now before going under contract and getting an appraisal only for that appraisal to be $40k to $60k or more under list price. I can tell you that as a lender, when a home comes in $60k under list price (and it has happened!!!) and you ask the Real Estate Agent to give you comps to support the value so that you can challenge the appraisal…and they don't have any…that is a huge mistake. You have just wasted everyone's time and the buyers money, and you potentially just cost yourself a sale. The last thing you want to do is have unhappy buyers, sellers, agents and lenders. When making an offer you must consider these things.

Pull Comparable Sales ("comps"). You must see what has recently SOLD; do not make your decision on Active comps. Sold comps will be used to determine Market Value.

When Reviewing comps, you want to look within a 1 mile radius for homes that are similar in Age, Square Footage, Bedrooms/Bathrooms and similar features like a Pool, Waterfront, Golf Course View, etc.

Know the Price Per Square Foot and the List Price to Sales Price Ratio to avoid a low offer. When you are doing the Buyer Presentation you want to explain to your buyers how it works. You may have buyers from other areas or other countries where it is very common to offer 20% under market value or under list price. If you are able to show your buyers what the average List Price to Sales Price Ratio is and you can explain what the average is for your area, you will avoid lowball offers or refuse to make lowball offers based off the Average List Price to Sales Price Ratio for the area.

Include a Pre-Approval Letter or Proof of Funds. From the beginning of the Buyer Presentation you must explain that either of these are needed before you can make a proper offer. In most areas, an offer will not be accepted without one or the other. Prepare them for that during the Buyer Presentation.

Multiple Offer Situation

Depending on the market and the price point, there may be times when you are in a Multiple Offer Situation. If that is the case for you, you will want to look at your offer to see how you can make it stronger. Can you shorten the timeframe for the Home Inspection Period or the closing date? Can you make the offer a cash offer because you have a slam dunk Pre-Approval? Can you go in with your highest and best offer and make the terms more favorable? What can you do to make your offer the most appealing to the Seller and Listing Agent.... Which brings me to my last and final point.

Present the offer in person. So, this sounds insane...and I have mixed feelings about this. I have never done this but it has happened to me. The very first listing I took when moving to Miami, I underpriced the property. It happens!!! My phone was blowing up. I had a day full of scheduled showings and at least 15 offers. One of the agents called me and asked to present her offer in person with my sellers there!?!?! I had no idea what to do and this was my first deal in Miami. Honestly, I thought maybe this was the norm? Anyways, I agreed.

This seasoned agent came to my office; me and my sellers were present in the conference room. The Buyer Agent not only presented her offer in person, but gave us the sob story and a letter from her buyers as to why they really wanted the home. Now they were not the highest offer, BUT my sellers took that offer because it became personal. If you are in a Multiple Offer Situation or with a Seller that will not budge, consider making an offer in person OR having your buyers write a letter or an email as to why they want the house. You never know; that may seal the deal!!!

If you want a Step by Step Plan and want to create a buyer presentation, take the Buyers class at www.realestatesecretsunlocked.com and don't forget to checkout our Facebook Community at Realtors Guide to Mass Production.

Chapter 8

Designing Your Life

As I sit here and write the last chapter of this book, I am reflecting on my life in the past and in my business. I realized that I had accidentally designed my life. You might be thinking, so what does that mean?

Basically, it means that when I was in Real Estate I was not the "norm." Not because I purposely tried to NOT be the "norm" but there was no other choice.

After the Crash …yes the major crash…of 2007 to 2009, I had just had two babies. My daughter in August 2007 and my son in December 2008. I knew I had to work. Not only did I have to work but I had to get My Hustle on and Bust My Butt to survive. I had two choices, crawl into a hole…pretend this was not happening and probably sink into deep depression...OR...get my Butt out of bed every day, bright and early before my husband and kids even woke up, do some form of exercise, plan my day, jump on the phone with my role-play partners and get to work! I choose option 2.

The thing is, I also had these two babies and wanted to make sure I spent time with them, so I figured out how to create a Real Estate business working Monday through Thursday, with a ½ day on Friday. Now, I am not going to say I didn't work nights and weekends. I did work nights Monday through Thursday, but it was work from home on my computer.... not out showing properties. I rarely worked weekends and if I did, it was maybe a few hours on a Saturday or Sunday. Most people get into real estate and don't think about how they want to plan their day or week and how to structure their schedule so that the business fits within the life they want to live.

Gary Keller talks about a Life By Design. You need to Design Your Life. Not only in Real Estate but in your Personal Life, too.

Ask yourself, are you satisfied with your life? If you were at the end of your life and were looking back, did you accomplish everything you were set out to do in this world? Did all of your hopes and dreams come true? If the answer is no than start today! Design Your Life so you can do everything you were meant to do in your lifetime.

Figure out what you want in life, what is important to you, how you want to design this business and what your ideal day looks like; then figure out what clients you want to go after. If you do not design your life, others will design it for you. You will become Re-Active. You will jump in the car whenever a buyer wants to see a home while feeling terrible that you are missing your kids or grandkids birthday party. But, you think you have to do it this way because, "someone needs to pay the bills."

I want you to think long and hard about the life you want to live and what that means to you. How do you want to design your life and how do you want to make this business fit and work with the life you want? Do not think that, as a Real Estate Agent, the norm is to spend nights and weekends carting buyers around or showing your listings. It is time to take control of your life. I am sure you got into Real Estate because you saw an opportunity. An opportunity to have the flexibility in your day and the opportunity to make unlimited amounts of money.

When you are in the trenches, often you can start to lose hope or the opportunity you once saw feels impossible. Don't feel that way. I encourage you to get a journal and write down your Dreams and Goals. Then Believe in Yourself and Believe that you can accomplish Everything you set out to accomplish. Come up with a Plan on how you are going to achieve it. Take small steps every day to do something to get you closer to your goal. Be Pro-Active and not Re-Active. I know this book just scratches the surface for Real Estate Agents and your business. If you are looking for more in depth trainings I created a website at www.realestatesecretsunlocked.com to help you in your journey. Check out the classes for a more in depth look at each aspect of the Real Estate sales business and get ready to take your business to the next level. I guarantee that if you Dream It and you Believe It, you will Achieve It! Go out there and be the Rockstar that you are! Dream, Believe, Achieve!

References

Immediate Action Steps:

Go to www.realestatesecretsunlocked.com and checkout the Following-

Vault for the Free Downloads and Working PDFs that go along with this book

Video Trainings for a More In-Depth Look at Each Chapter & Soon To Come Online Training Courses

Resources to help you in your Business. This section has recommendations on different things like CRM's, Lead Generating Systems, Database Management and so much more!

Request to be a Member of Realtors Guide to Mass Production and Believe Learn Achieve Facebook Pages

Check Out my Youtube Channel at Believe Learn Achieve for Training and Inspirational Videos!

Dream * Believe* Learn * Achieve!

DANIELLE DAMIANOV

www.ingramcontent.com/pod-product-compliance
Lightning Source LLC
Chambersburg PA
CBHW071408210526
45465CB00001B/300